Born into a wealthy Boston banking family, the nephew of J. P. Morgan, Harry Crosby was the very embodiment of flaming youth in the Roaring Twenties. A recipient of the Croix de Guerre for heroism in the American Ambulance Corps in World War One, he sustained trauma that fueled his extravagant and restlessly experimental expatriate lifestyle with his wife Caresse in Paris, before taking his life and that of his mistress in a notorious double suicide in a New York City hotel room in 1929. The Crosbys' Black Sun Press was famed for its elegantly designed limited editions, publishing first editions of important works of modernism, including Hart Crane's *The Bridge,* and the first excerpts of Joyce's *Work-In-Progress* to appear in book form. Crosby's own poetry has been little seen since its original publication in books by the Black Sun Press, the last of which appeared in 1931. Now acclaimed editor and poet Ben Mazer has brought together all of Crosby's contemporary magazine and anthology appearances, as well as drawing on poems from five of Crosby's collections, to present the first authorized edition of Crosby's poems to appear in book form since 1931.

Praise for Harry Crosby's work

"Harry has a great, great gift. He has a wonderful gift of carelessness."
—Ernest Hemingway to Archibald MacLeish

"It is a glimpse of chaos not reduced to order. But the chaos alive, not the chaos of matter. A glimpse of the living, untamed chaos."
—DH Lawrence on Harry Crosby's poetry

"Of course one can 'go too far' and except in directions in which we can go too far there is no interest in going at all; and only those who will risk going too far can possibly find out just how far one can go. Not to go far enough is to remain 'in the vague' as surely and less creditably than to exceed. Indeed, the mentors of pseudo-classicism should consistently content themselves with agnosticism, or at most with the simple faith of Islam; for no extravagance of a genuine poet can go so far over the borderline of ordinary intellect as the Creeds of the Church. And the poet who fears to take the risk that what he writes may turn out not to be poetry at all, is a man who has surely failed, who ought to have adopted some less adventurous vocation."
—T. S. Eliot, in the preface to *Transit of Venus*

"I think you have got hold of something valuable in *Transit of Venus* … you hit upon a kind of true brevity in these and other poems. And that brevity is signed with your name … I think you have learned the smell of your own flesh. I think you should be satisfied …"
—Archibald MacLeish in a letter to Harry Crosby

"I never met anyone who was so imbued with literature; he was drowned in it."
—Archibald MacLeish

"Your particular politics of existence, being so much more consistent—and without complaint—than most, could save at least a generation from despair."
—Kay Ryan in a letter to Crosby

"To us, the difficulty with the sonnet seems that the questions invited are such that it is hardly surprising no answer is given. And if we may put our own question, is the rhyme of the last line of 'Study for a Soul' permissible?"
—*Atlantic Monthly* in a rejection letter to Crosby

"… undoubtedly one of the most beautiful, and at the same time seethingly denunciatory voices of the time … Crosby was another Rimbaud, but a more engaging literary personality."
—Norman MacLeod, *Morada* literary magazine

"… a rare and delicate spirit, his clear eyes unblinded by wealth, his Muse untarnished by the fool's gold of commercialism, we shall not look on his like again …"
—Jack Conroy, *The Rebel Poet* literary magazine

"… to be living now, to be living, alive and full of the thing, to believe in the sun, the moon or the stars; or whatever is your belief, and to write of these things with an alertness sharp as a blade and as relentless, is a challenge that is the solemn privilege of the young. In any generation there are but few grave enough to acknowledge this responsibility. In ours Harry Crosby stands singularly alone …"
—Kay Boyle in *transition* magazine

"Living near Harry Crosby was like the experience of an equatorial springtime, when the tyrant Sun, lord of life and death, strikes dazzling down, summoning from the four horizons storm-clouds and thunder and cyclone, when the scorched soil quakes and crumbles and life is fevered almost to frenzy, in strained expectancy of the monsoon."
—Stuart Gilbert

Selected Poems

Selected Poems
by Harry Crosby

Deluxe Illustrated Edition
Edited and with an introduction by
Ben Mazer

MadHat Press
Cheshire, Massachusetts

MadHat Press
Cheshire, Massachusetts

Copyright © 2020 Ben Mazer
All rights reserved

The Library of Congress has assigned
this edition a Control Number of
2020940215

ISBN 978-1-952335-06-8 (deluxe illustrated edition)

Cover design by Marc Vincenz
Illustrations by Alastair (Baron Hans Henning von Voigt)
Book design by MadHat Press

www.madhat-press.com

First Printing

List of Illustrations

illustration by Alastair from *Red Skeletons*	*frontispiece*
photo of Harry Crosby in WWI uniform	xviii
illustration by Alastair from *Red Skeletons*	2
photo of Harry Crosby	46
photo of Caresse Crosby and her whippet, Clitoris	70
photo of Harry Crosby in the sun	110
wedding photo of Harry and Caresse Crosby	126
photo of Kay Boyle and Harry Crosby	146
illustration by Alastair from *Red Skeletons*	159
illustration by Alastair from *Red Skeletons*	174

Table of Contents

Introduction by Ben Mazer   xix

Poems from *transition*

HAIL : DEATH !	3
SUITE	
AERONAUTICS	5
THE SUN	8
THE NEW WORD	12
OBSERVATION-POST	13
DREAMS 1928–1929	24
FOR A PROTECTION	31
ILLUSTRATIONS OF MADNESS	32
SHORT INTRODUCTION TO THE WORD	35
SLEEPING TOGETHER	
FOR A PROTECTION	37
WHITE SLIPPER	37
WHITE CLOVER	37
SAFETY-PIN	38
HUMAN FLESH AND GOLDEN APPLES	38
I BREAK WITH THE PAST	39
GOLDEN SPOON	39
AUNT AGATHA	40
IT IS SNOWING	40
WHITE AEROPLANES IN FLIGHT	41
MIRACULOUS MESSAGE	41
EMBRACE ME YOU SAID	42
A PROGRESS UPWARD	42
WHITE FIRE	43
REVIRGINATE	43
ANIMAL MAGNETISM	43

Poems from *The Decachord, Blues, The Morada, Pagany,* and Four Anthologies

OUR LADY OF TEARS.	47

BILITIS	48
TRUMPET OF DEPARTURE	49
SCORN	51
DESOLATE	52
103°	53
ASSASSIN	54
THE ROSE	58
OUR FEET	59
SLEEPING TOGETHER	60
SHARING FIRE	61
ROOTS	62
COEUR DE JEUNE FEMME	63
VENUS	64
MIRACLE	65
RECKON THE DAYS	66
INVOCATION TO THE SUN-GODDESS	67
SCORN	68

SLEEPING TOGETHER : A BOOK OF DREAMS

INSPECTION	69
GIRLS UNDER TEN	69
ON THE GROUNDS OF INDECENCY	70
WE HAVE FORGOTTEN OUR CALLING-CARDS	70
NO INDICATION OF WHERE I MIGHT FIND YOU	70
GAME OF TAG	71
PERFORMANCE BY TWO	71
I AM IN YOUR SOUL	72
UNREMOVED BY RUBBING	72
MOSQUITO	73
OVID'S FLEA	73
CAT	73

GAZELLE AT LUNCHEON	74
THEY THE TWELVE LIONS	74
ONE HUNDRED WAYS OF KISSING GIRLS	75
SUNRISE EXPRESS	75
I HAD NO IDEA WHAT THEY WOULD DO NEXT	75
HE CALLED US A GIRL	76
MIRACULOUS MESSAGE	76
WHITE AEROPLANES IN FLIGHT	77
ANIMAL MAGNETISM	77
SAINT VALENTINE'S NIGHT	77
YOUR EYES ARE THE REAL EYES	78
NAKED LADY IN A YELLOW HAT	78
CUE OF WIND	78
CC 78	
IT IS SNOWING	79
VERY NICE TO LOOK AT AND SWEET TO TOUCH	79
YOU ARE STANDING ON YOUR HEAD	80
STREET OF THE FOUR WINDS	80
QUEEN OF HEARTS	81
WHITE ERMINE	81
MIRACLE OF THE TOOTH	82
C PREFERRED	82
A PROGRESS UPWARD	82
THE RED UMBRELLA	83
I WAS NEVER HAPPIER	83
SAFETY-PIN	83
SOLUTION OF A MYSTERY	84
REVIRGINATE	84
HUMAN FLESH AND GOLDEN APPLES	85
AERONAUTICS	85
GIRLS ARE CLIMBING	85

YOU WERE TRYING TO TELL ME SOMETHING	86
THE CRAMOISY QUEEN	86
DICE IN A YELLOW SKULL	87
WHITE CLOVER	87
CRUEL MOUTH AND LITTLE EAR	88
I FOLLOW YOU TO BED	88
FOR THE PREVENTION OF CRUELTY TO BRIDES	89
I BREAK WITH THE PAST	89
GOLDEN SPOON	90
SEESAW	90
FOR A PROTECTION	90
WHITE FIRE	91
AUNT AGATHA	91
RITZ TOWER	92
WHITE STOCKINGS	92
WHITE SLIPPER	92
ONE LETTER OF THE ALPHABET	93
IN PURSUIT OF YOUR EYES	93
Horse Race	94
Invocation to the Mad Queen	96
In Madness	97
Empty Bed Blues	98
Water-Lilies	99
Quatrains to the Sun	100
Sunstroke	102

Poems from *Chariot of the Sun* (1928)

STUDY FOR A SOUL	109
SUN RHAPSODY	110
TOUGGOURT	111
PHOTOHELIOGRAPH	112

TREE OF GOLD	113
PSYCHOPATHIA SEXUALIS	115
FRAGMENT OF AN ETUDE FOR A SUN-DIAL	116

Poems from *Transit of Venus* (1929)

FIRST MEETING	125
ALTAZIMUTH	126
YOU CAME TO ME	127
POEM	128
YOUTH	129
YOUR KISS	130
BE NOT IT IS I	131
WERE IT NOT BETTER	132
PRAYER	133
THAT HARD WORD	134
LOST THINGS	135
BEAUTY IN BED	136
LITTLE POEMS	137
KISS	138
FIRE-EATERS	139
FORECAST	140
AND MEMORY	141
YES	142

Poems from *Torchbearer* (1931)

ACADEMY OF STIMULANTS	145
TATTOO	146
I DRINK TO THE SUN	147
ASSASSIN	148
FOR YOU	150
INFURIATE	151

UNLEASH THE HOUNDS	152
STRONG FOR BATTLE	153
GLADNESS	154
ALLEGORY	155
TIDAL WAVE	156
Textual Notes	157
Bibliography	171
Acknowledgments	175
About the Editor	177

Harry Crosby in WWI uniform

Introduction

It is sometimes said that poetry can kill a man, that, to the poet, poetry is a matter of life and death. Countless poets have encountered early or tragic death, many of them suicides: suicides from madness, from depression, from poverty, trauma, and even from belief in the hierarchal absolute of poetry. Rimbaud called for a derangement of the senses; many heeded the call, not least among them Harry Crosby, who, unlike Rimbaud, was wealthy, had already had his senses deranged by his war experiences, and was living with PTSD and mania. Crosby revered Rimbaud, and with Rimbaud's self-deregulation in mind, believed in his own idealizations of suicide. To his wife, Caresse Crosby, he had proposed suicide pacts on several occasions since early in their relationship. He wrote about such pacts in his poems and in his diaries, and he talked about them, most consequentially, with the most significant of his many mistresses, Josephine Rotch Bigelow, with whom he was found dead in bed—a bullet hole to her left temple, a bullet hole to his right temple, his right hand holding a .25 caliber pistol, his free hand joined in Josephine's—in a New York hotel room on December 11, 1929. The couple was fully clothed, and there was no suicide note. They had consumed immense quantities of gin and opium pills, not unusual for Harry, or his "fire-princess", as he called Josephine, who, like himself, was thoroughly a product of Back Bay Boston. Had Josephine been the first to call Harry's bluff, and insist that he carry through in action the belief he expressed to her, that the greatest expression and fulfillment of love was for two lovers to die together in suicide? But where had the belief come from? Had it come from the derangement of his senses? Was he driven to suicide, as he was to the fatal calling of the poet, by his close experiences of death, violence and carnage in the first world war, experiences which drove his manic sexual drive, his commitment to poetry, to madness, to drugs and gambling, horses and medieval mills, Sun-worship, aviation, and books, while becoming one of the most elite and legendary publishers of the century with his and Caresse's Black Sun Press in Paris? When one thinks of Harry Crosby, one thinks of youth aflame, mad for love, drugs, poetry, speed, flight, tragic fatality, Sun-worship. One thinks of the enormous amounts of money that enabled him to live such a bigger-than-the-movies life. One thinks of the gruesome scenes and traumatic experiences that he witnessed in World War One as an ambulance driver. Old friends, and those who knew him intimately, thought the war was ticking away like a time-bomb in Harry.

Henry Grew Crosby was born in Back Bay Boston on June 4, 1898, the son and heir of a wealthy banking family; his mother's brother was J. Pierpont Morgan, Jr.; his father was a direct descendent of Alexander Hamilton. At St. Mark's, the prescribed preparation for Harvard, Harry was a bit of a prankster, and excelled at track, but was mostly seen as a loner. Upon graduation in 1916, he enlisted in the American Ambulance Corps and by late June was in France. Soon he experienced heavy battle conditions at Verdun, and saw gore that would impress him for life. He carried buckets of limbs. He wrote home:

> I saw the most gruesome sight I've ever seen. Lying on a blood-stained brancard was a man—not older than twenty I afterwards ascertained—suffering the agonies of hell. His whole right cheek was completely shot away so you could see all the insides of his face. He had no jaws, teeth, or lips left. His nose was plastered in. Blood was streaming all over.

Then a shell exploded ten yards away from him, and he miraculously escaped being killed by jumping to the floor of his ambulance. He wrote his parents that on that day he had turned from a boy into a man. Somehow he was no longer afraid of death.

When he returned from France in 1919, a recipient of his treasured Croix de Guerre, he entered Harvard to take an accelerated war degree, and pleased his father by unenthusiastically making A.D. among Harvard's final clubs. He didn't make much of an impression at Harvard, and if he was interested in literature, nobody noticed it.

Before the end of his career at Harvard (he graduated in the spring of 1921), on July 4, 1920, Harry met, through the innocence of his mother, Polly Peabody, or Mrs. Richard Rogers Peabody, fell in love with her immediately, and within weeks was having sex with her and entreating her to divorce her husband and marry him. He wrote her:

> I promise you that whenever you want we shall die together and what's more I am perfectly ready now or will be anytime. With the absolute Faith that we shall be One in Heaven as soon as we die forever.

He obsessed on this theme in letters, offering it as a solution if she couldn't get a divorce, even offering to kill her and then kill himself so that she "wouldn't have to take the blame".

Late in May 1921, Richard Peabody offered Polly a divorce, and they began a trial separation of six months. Polly promised her mother not to see Harry. Toward the end of the year Harry took a job with the Shawmut National Bank to please his father, and Polly began accepting weekend visits from him in New York. On January 1, 1922, Harry began to keep his diaries, later published as *Shadows of the Sun* in three volumes (1928; 1929; 1930) by The Black Sun Press.

By March 14 he had resigned from the bank. A week later his mother secured him a job at the family bank in Paris. The Boston society columns wrote that the family and friends of the Crosbys hoped that Harry's separation from Polly would break up their engagement, which had scandalized Boston. But Polly went to Paris to be with Harry, only to leave for America abruptly when Harry had an affair with another woman from Boston. Harry cursed himself in his diary. Finally, he wired Polly that he couldn't stand one more day without her and that he was coming to America and wanted her to meet him. She wired back, "YES", and they were married on September 9, 1922, in New York City. The couple, with Polly's two young children, took up residence in Paris, and Harry continued his bank work at Morgan, Harjes. The first mention of poetry in Harry's diary had been on April 17, when he had quoted from Baudelaire. Harry quit the bank at the very end of 1923; he wanted to be a poet. He had begun an intense friendship with his father's cousin, Walter Van Rensselaer Berry (1859–1927), an international lawyer and man of the world who was friends with Henry James and Marcel Proust, and Edith Wharton's writing master (she wanted to marry him, but he wouldn't capitulate), an esteemed gentleman in Parisian social and literary circles. It was Berry who encouraged Harry to leave the bank and write. As Walter Berry was an ornament to the family and its values, Harry wrote home triumphantly of Cousin Berry's advice to him, which was received with perplexed incomprehension. Harry sank himself into studies of the French poets that Berry admired: Valéry, Verlaine, Baudelaire, and above all Rimbaud. It was around this time that Harry began his course of Sun-worship, influenced by Berry's obsession with Egypt. It was in April of 1925 that Harry and Polly announced to Berry that Polly would henceforth be known as "Caresse". The name had been chosen to adorn Polly's first book of poems, *Crosses of Gold,* which was being privately printed. Berry passed away in August 1927, and left his enormous collection of rare books to Harry and to Edith Wharton, with Harry in the end receiving the lion's share of the countless exotic volumes. The books arrived on May 4, 1928; Harry wrote in his diary:

> Books Books Books Books eight thousand of them crate after crate crate after crate borne upon the shoulders of solid men came cascading all morning and all afternoon into the house and my library is a pyramid of books and C's atelier is stacked high with books (I hope the ceiling won't fall through) and the staircase is blocked with books and the guest room is blocked with books and the front hall is blocked with books—books books books and what books!—a leaf from the Gutenberg Bible two chained manuscripts from a monastery

an illuminated Koran illuminated Psalm books an enormous Book of the Dead (the largest book I have ever seen) the first edition of de Quincey's Opium Eater bound by Zaehnsdorf the rare first edition of Les Liasons Dangereuses a microscopic volume of old French songs (the smallest book I have ever seen) the Sacred Books of the East in fifty volumes an Histoire Naturelle in one hundred and twenty seven volumes a magnificent set of Casanova with erotic plates superb sets of Bacon of the Decameron of Beaumont and Fletcher of Audubon of Henry James of Maupassant of the Arabian Nights of Orlando Furioso books from the Aldine Press from the Elzevir Press from the Plantin Press books of Ancient Travel (Marco Polo Hakluyt Tavernier and the more modern Arabia Deserta) books containing priceless maps books on art (enough to constitute a library in itself) books with the bindings and arms of the Kings of France books with the arms of Mazarin of Richelieu of Napoleon of Madame de Pompadour of Le Roi Soleil and the signatures of Le Roi Soleil and of Henry Fourth and of Voltaire and of Alexander Pope Italian Books French Books English Books Spanish Books Books in Latin Books in Greek every kind of Book imaginable from the oldest Incunabula down to the most recent number of Transition for which treasures I offer thanks to Cousin Walter on the Book of the Dead and in the name of the Sun.

Much else happened between 1925 and 1928. There were parties, racehorses (bet on and purchased), travel through North Africa (where Harry smoked hashish), endless perusal of books, and much smoking of opium. There were also Harry's many sexual liasons, though Caresse was always his favorite. Caresse, in turn, had affairs of her own. Harry and Caresse set the tone of the Four Arts

Ball in Paris each year. One year the theme was Inca. Harry dressed in a loincloth, his body covered in red chalk, wearing a necklace of dead pigeons. Caresse made her entrance bare-breasted, riding a giant paper dragon carried by students.

Then there was Harry's self-education as a poet. He was enamoured of the Symbolists and the Decadents. His favorite poets were Rimbaud, Baudelaire, T. S. Eliot, E. E. Cummings, and James Joyce. He read Wilde's *The Picture of Dorian Gray* three times, copying out long passages from it in his diary. Caresse taught him how to write sonnets in 1924, and by 1925 he had enough for a book, *Sonnets for Caresse*, which the couple had privately printed, laying the beginnings of The Black Sun Press. It wasn't until the publication of Harry's second book of poems, *Red Skeletons*, in 1927, that Harry and Caresse were to assume a name as a publishing house, Editions Narcisse, and, working for the first time with the printer Roger Lescaret, were to direct the design of their books. It was here that they first showed a flair for choice types, adequate margins, fine papers, interesting bindings, and innovative design, printed in tiny editions, often numbered in purple pencil. *Red Skeletons* fit this model. There were 33 copies on Japon Impérial (numbered one through 33), 333 copies on vergé de Hollande (numbered 34 through 366), and four copies with unique frontispiece designs executed by the artists Alastair, Constance Comtesse and Jumilhac, on various papers, for close friends and for the Crosbys. The title-page bore a skull-and-crossbones. George Minkoff, bibliographer of The Black Sun Press, examined a copy "bound in black morocco with the Crosby crest on the front and back", and the spine printed in gold, and speculated: "Possibly all hors de commerce copies were so bound." A year later Crosby was dissatisfied by the book, and burned the remaining 80 unsold copies in a bonfire, shooting the four copies that didn't burn to pieces with a shotgun. It was around this time that Crosby began to show what poetic maturity marked the few brief remaining years of his violently short life. This mature period of Crosby's poetry marks the volumes *Chariot of the Sun* (1928), *Transit of Venus* (1928; 1929 second edition, with added poems), *Mad Queen* (1929), *Sleeping Together* (1929), and *Torchbearer* (1931, published posthumously with Notes by Ezra Pound). It is from these five books that almost all of the poems in this edition have been drawn, though I have given every magazine and anthology text of these poems, as well as having drawn directly upon three of these collections.

In an unpublished portion of his diary, probably written in his last days, Harry wrote:

> Transit of Venus (for Josephine)
> Sleeping Together (for Caresse)
> (these are the two books I have written which
> are damn good the others can go to hell)

Included in this collection are 61 of the 64 poems in *Sleeping Together*, represented by the posthumous selection of the editors of *American Caravan* IV (1931). 35 poems from *Sleeping Together* are here reprinted from *transition* as well, with some overlap. This is both to preserve the historical record of Harry's career as seen through his magazine and anthology appearances, and because the poems exist in greatly or at least significantly rewritten versions, which can be seen by comparing the poems in *transition* with the same poems in *American Caravan* IV. This edition consists of 5 main sections: Poems from *transition*; Poems from the *Decachord, Blues, The Morada, Pagany*, and Four Anthologies; Poems from *Chariot of the Sun* (1928); Poems from *Transit of Venus* (1929); and Poems from *Torchbearer* (1931). The poems in the first two sections make up the whole of Harry Crosby's output in magazines and anthologies. This represents a historical record not only of what was seen at the time, but also of what was submitted and what was selected for publication. Harry's magazine output took place during the years 1928–1929, the last two years of his life, and the years of his most exciting poetry. He had the adoration and trust of the Editor of *transition*, Eugene Jolas, to whom he gave a free hand in editing, changing or ordering his work, but who is not likely to have wittingly changed anything, beyond what would be changed through the processes of selecting and ordering. The posthumous publication of the *Sleeping Together* sequence in *transition* in 1930 was probably directed by Caresse Crosby.

What was Crosby's poetry like? Surely there has long been a need for an edition like this one, for the scarce Black Sun Press books of Harry's have long since disappeared into archives and into the hands of collectors. Since the original Black Sun editions, Crosby's poems have simply not been available for perusal since 1931, with the exception of a scanty and generally ill-chosen smattering of his poetry sprinkled through Geoffrey Wolff's biography *Black Sun* (1976) and Edward Germain's Black Sparrow edition of Crosby's diaries, *Shadows of the Sun* (1977), which quote from Crosby's immature sonnets, and some of his more violent and notorious tirades; nine rather more well-chosen poems appear in Jerome Rothenberg's anthology *Revolution of the Word* (1974; second edition 2004). This present edition aims to give a generous selection of Crosby's most interesting, authoritative, and representative poems.

Two of the marks of the true poet are singularity and authenticity. Spending whole days doing nothing but reading, turning out poem after poem in wild outbursts of energy, and laboring for hours over the revision of his work, Crosby had both. He had the singularity of a voice that sounds like no other. There is an Eliotic significance, a metaphysical fusion of the senses with the intellect, a sense of a cutting seriousness infusing the poetry. There was the authenticity of one who means, as a matter of life or death, every word that he writes. When these two marks are fused, work comes violently to life, incomprehensible but compelling, something each reader might interpret or experience differently. Although Crosby's early work in *Sonnets for Caresse* and *Red Skeletons* was contrived and derivative, apprentice work, the poems he wrote in the last two years of his life, 1928–1929, the years of a perhaps psychotic division of allegiances between Caresse Crosby and Josephine Noyes Rotch, were marked by a maturity of expression, an ability to fuse the elements of poetry. Looking at the poems alone, apart from the legendary biography, may be a reason to find more in them than was found during the years of their publication.

There is a divergence of styles in those last few Black Sun Press books. The poems in *Sleeping Together*, little-punctuated short prose poems, are surrealist in nature. The poems of *Mad Queen* and *Torchbearer* are more violent tirades. *Transit of Venus* presents extremely short, mostly unpunctuated poems in verse, terse and cryptic monographs on the madness of love. Take for example the poem "First Meeting":

> When you are the flower
> I am the shadow cast by the flower
> When I am the fire
> You are the mirror reflecting the fire
> And when Venus has entered the disk of the Sun
> Then you are that Venus and I am the Sun.

The poems are strange yet original, perhaps crazy, for Harry Crosby was a man who was crazed—"half sane half insane" (*Shadows of the Sun*). As a poet he was possessed, certainly by the influence of Rimbaud, and in general the French poets from Baudelaire, or perhaps Villon, down to the surrealists whom he brushed shoulders with. He was possessed by worship of the Sun, by opium, by danger, by the impulse to make extravagant gestures, by sexual mania, by visions of a desired death and suicide (the only question being, when was the right moment). But what made it authentic, however childish, however given to incompletion or vagueness, however tiresome the repetitive symbols like incessant chants, was that Crosby had the conviction of his belief. As T. S. Eliot recognized, Crosby had a need to write in symbols, to effect his campaign around a tom-tom-beat background of key phrases and vocables. To manifest one's poetry through symbols was to seek after a solid truth that one could hang on to, even if another might not share one's belief. Need another share it, if Eliot can posit that true poetry can only strike and affect each separate reader differently?

The Crosbys directed Lescaret in the printing of Harry's *Chariot of the Sun* (1928), too, under the imprint "At the Sign of the Sundial". But with the publication of *Shadows of the Sun*, on June 4, 1928, Harry's 30th birthday, a book bearing the imprint of The Black Sun Press was for the first time issued into the world.

It was not only fine bookmaking which propelled The Black Sun Press to fame. It was also the list. Among the books published by The Black Sun Press were *Sun* by D.H. Lawrence (1928), *Short Stories* by Kay Boyle (1929), *Tales Told of Shem and Shaun* by James Joyce (1929; three episodes in what was then known as *Work-in-Progress*, and the first selection from *Work-in-Progress* to appear in book form), *Einstein* by Archibald MacLeish (1929), *The Escaped Cock* by D. H. Lawrence (1929), *The Bridge* by Hart Crane, with photographs by Walker Evans (1930), and *Imaginary Letters* by Ezra Pound (1930). Artists such as Alastair, Marie Laurencin, Max Ernst, Polia Chentoff, Paul Émile Bécat, Walker Evans, Caresse Crosby, and even D. H. Lawrence, contributed illustrations and designs to Black Sun Press books in the years 1928–1931. Harry must have felt an elevation of esteem in his relationship with his parents, fooling around with book publishing, which to his parents must have had the hint of commerce about it, even if none of the words in the books could be understood. Perhaps the publishing enterprise gave them pause to think that Harry wasn't wholly crazy.

The height of the Crosbys' experience with The Black Sun Press was working with James Joyce on the numerous successive proofs to which Joyce subjected his text and the Crosbys during the course of preparing *Tales Told of Shem and Shaun* for publication. Harry, to whom Joyce was a God, was buoyant at the experience of hearing Joyce explain all the changes and additions he was making to the text. Caresse went to see Picasso, to ask him for a frontispiece portrait of Joyce for the book. Picasso declined, on the grounds that he never did commissioned work. Besides, he wasn't interested in Joyce. Brancusi wound up creating the frontispiece, a portrait of Joyce in zigzag lines. Joyce didn't care for it.

Meanwhile other forces were shaping up. "Enter the Youngest Princess of the Sun!" reads Harry's diary entry for June 9, 1928. That day he had met twenty-year-old Josephine Noyes Rotch at the Lido. She came from a prominent Boston family, and was in Europe to pick out her trousseau, as she had become engaged two weeks earlier to Albert Smith Bigelow, also of Boston. Harry and his "Fire Princess" made the most of the eight days they had together in Venice. After returning to America, Josephine sent cables to Harry almost every day, and on the last day of July wired: "DO NOT

BE DEPRESSED. TAKE THE NEXT BOAT. YOU KNOW I LOVE YOU AND WANT YOU." Harry couldn't bring himself to do it, and risk losing Caresse. By the third week in August, he had written fifty-two poems for *Transit of Venus*, his Josephine book.

It was around this time that the Crosbys took a twenty-year lease on a medieval mill in Ermenonville, an hour away from Paris. The mill, which they bought for quiet and work, was soon opened to parades of revelers: royalty, movie stars (Douglas Fairbanks and Mary Pickford), poets (notably Hart Crane, visiting France on money given to him by the philanthropist Otto Kahn, and whose long, unfinished poem, *The Bridge*, Harry would soon offer to publish in a limited Black Sun Press edition), artists (Salvador Dali was a frequent visitor), nuts of all stripes. In Gatsby-like scenes, unknown wits might be found wandering around half-naked the morning after a particularly raucous party, or six might take to one bed together, one of them a complete stranger.

On November 17, 1928, Harry and Caresse docked in New York. In Boston on November 26, Harry wrote in his diary: "the best part of the evening was the voice of fire over the wire." On December 7, the day the Crosbys were supposed to sail back to France, Harry vacillated as to whether or not to sail, and finally decided to remain behind in New York while Caresse returned to France; he would not rejoin her in Paris until Christmas eve. On December 8, he wrote in his diary: "I am horribly depressed (O Christ why didn't I sail)". On January 29, 1929, he wrote in his diary: "wrote to the youngest Princess". On February 4: "there were fire-words from the Fire-Princess". On March 14: "I am influenced most by the Fire-Princess, by Rimbaud, by Blake, by Aknaton, by Van Gogh, by Marlowe." March 19: "wrote a letter to the Fire-Princess." May 28: "It was raining and I kept thinking of the Fire-Princess." August 27: "to-day a pure-gold letter from the Fire-Princess." October 19: "I haven't heard from the Fire-Princess for so long but she is mine—whether I hear from her or not has really very little importance." October 31: "Letter and a gold eagle and the sun from the Fire Princess I am glad Gold and Fire and Sun." On November 3, he finished writing *Sleeping Together* ("these dreams for C").

A notable occasion in Harry's life was when he witnessed Lindbergh's landing in Paris on May 20, 1927. On August 1, 1929, he decided that he wanted to learn how to fly. Soon he was taking lessons, and going up with an instructor. Then, he became more and more impatient as he yearned to be allowed to fly solo, but continued to be sent up with an instructor. He was determined to fly solo before departing for America. Finally, on Armistice Day, November 11, Harry completed his first solo flight. Five days later he and Caresse sailed for New York. On November 18, Harry received a radiogram from Josephine: "IMPATIENT." On November 22, the Crosbys docked in New York. The next day, Harry visited Josephine before the Harvard-Yale football game. Harry saw much of Josephine in the next two weeks. The final entry in Harry's diary reads:

> One is not in love unless one desires to die with one's beloved
>
> There is only one happiness it is to love and to be loved

—Ben Mazer

Poems from Transition

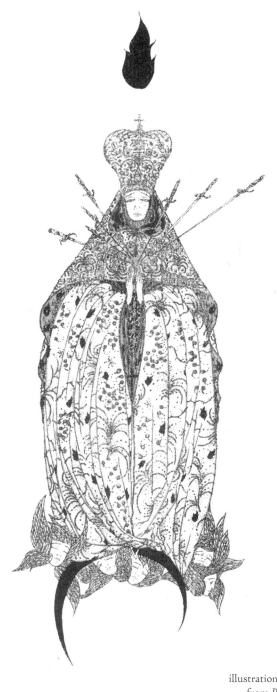

illustration by Alastair
from *Red Skeletons*

HAIL : DEATH !

Take the Gymnosophists who used to kill themselves in public in the market place ! Take the widows of India who flung themselves on the funeral pyres of their husbands ! Take the Greeks : Diogenes, Socrates, Demosthenes, Themistocles, and Sappho, because of her love for the disdainful Phaon. Take the Romans : Porcia, Arria, Lucretia, Brutus, and Cassius, and Cato !

Take Dido ! Take Cleopatra ! Take the Saints and Martyrs ! In a certain sense take Jesus Christ ! Take the Members of that famous Suicide Club, who drew lots once a year to see whose turn it was to die ! Take Modigliani ! Take Van Gogh, example of triumphant individuality, banner waving from the topmost pinnacle, and take his death into Sun ! Go to Van Gogh, you sluggards, consider his ways and be wise ! Take Nietzsche: " Die at the right time," no matter where you are, in the depths of the coal pit, in the crowded streets of the city, among the dunes of the desert, in cocktail bars, or in the perfumed corridors of the Ritz, at the right time, when your entire life, when your soul and your body, your spirit and your senses are concentrated, are reduced to a pin-point, the ultimate gold point, the point of finality, irrevocable as the sun, sun-point, then is the time, and not until then, and not after then (O horrors of anticlimax from which there is no recovering !) for us to penetrate into the cavern of the sombre Slave-Girl of Death, to enter upon coition with the sombre Slave-Girl of Death, to enjoy an orgasm with the sombre Slave-Girl of Death, in order to be reborn, in order to become what you wish to become, tree or flower or star or sun, or even dust and nothingness, for it is stronger to founder in the Black Sea of Nothingness, like a ship going down with flags, than to crawl like a Maldoror into the malodorous whore-house of evil and old age. Let not this be said of those who founder or those who, like red arrows, wing chaste and unafraid into the redgold of the Sun.

I recall the Hollow Men :

> " This is the way the world ends
> This is the way the world ends
> This is the way the world ends
> Not with a bang but a whimper ",

and Eliot is right, absolutely right, as regards the majority, as regards the stupid Philistines, whose lives have always been a whimper, whose lives could never be anything else but a whimper, whose lives must inevitably end with a whimper, they who prefer senility, who prefer putrefaction of the brain, who prefer hypocrisy, sterility, imbecility (do not confound with madness), impotence, to the strength and fury of a Sun-Death — dead bodies and dead souls dumped unceremoniously into the world's latrine.

But for the Seekers after Fire and the Seers and the Prophets (hail to you O men of transition !) and the Worshipers of the Sun, life ends not with a whimper, but with a Bang — a violent explosion mechanically perfect (" Imperthnthn thnthnthn "), while down and down downwards down down below with bloodied heaviness sinks the menstruous cloth of the past (protégez-vous contre la syphilis) for the eunuchs and the sabbatarians to feed upon (how can they know the Sun those dry trees, they of the clammy hands and the fetid breath, with their pro-cathedrals and their diplomacy ?). Let them devourdung, let their maggot fingers swarm over the red cloth, while we, having set fire to the powder-house of our souls, explode (suns within suns and cataracts of gold) into the frenzied fury of the Sun, into the madness of the Sun into the hot gold arms and hot gold eyes of the Goddess of the Sun!

[*transition* 14, Fall 1928]

SUITE

AERONAUTICS

A procession to the hill of Montmartre (where stand the famous windmills) in the midst of which is a large Balloon, mounted on wheels and drawn by two donkeys. Behind comes a monkey standing on its hind legs, in clerical garb, and a donkey both of them with trousers on, and looking happy. At the back is the personification of Fire on a cloud, holding a scroll in her hand on which are depicted two Balloons. The Balloon is in mid-air and is encircled by monkeys and donkeys waiting for the Ascent. A blind Man leaves the scene saying, I can see nothing. The Balloon is rising from the platform, in front of which is an enormous crowd of spectators. The Balloon has ascended into the atmosphere. The Balloon moves off in a horizontal direction. The Balloon has disappeared into space. An Explosion is heard. The Balloon has Exploded. The Balloon is on the ground and Peasants are attacking it with pitchforks. Landscape with cottage and hay barn and old white timber inn with thatched roof, men seated drinking, to left a farm-girl feeding pigs, waggoner with his horses at watertrough. The inn stands on the banks of the river behind spreading trees. A cow is drinking. The Virgin seated by the Tree. The Virgin with the Rabbits. Saint George with the Dragon. The Circumcision in the Stable. The Betrothal of the Virgin. The Wondrous Hog. The Brood Mares. The tiled buildings of the mill are seen on the further bank of the river. In foreground to right two women washing clothes. In centre soldiers firing. To left spectators with the American Flag above in various attitudes of alarm. A vixen sits on the ledge of the bank and looks toward five cubs, a sixth cub peers out of a hole in the bank. Enter the Blind Man. Enter an Aardvark. Enter a man with a knife left hand raised to his face (female figure partly nude floating in the air beside him). He is followed by a young woman plucking a fowl. Her hair is in curls she has pearls round her neck and she is wearing an ermine cloak with jewels. Enter a young peasant girl carrying basket rejecting the advances of a young man in uniform (female figure partly nude floating in the air beside him). Enter mother and child (the child has pyelitis). Enter Elsa de Brabant. Enter an Auger observing Birds. Enter a Flying Fox. Enter a Stork and a Pelican. Enter a Black Hawk. Enter a Red Swan. Enter Santa Claus with a portion of caviar. Enter Tilden. Enter Walter Hagen in a knitgrip knicker (no buckles to buckle). Enter the Tenth Plague of Egypt. Enter the Madonna of the Sleeping Cars. Enter Anna Livia Plurabelle. Enter La Mère Gérard. Enter La Vieille aux Loques. Enter La Marchande de Montarde. Enter the Red Dress. Enter two girls one combing her hair. Oh ! Why ! — I don't know about loving him very much. Enter Daniel Webster. Thank God ! I — I also — am an American ! Enter Christ and the Woman of Samaria. Enter the Man in the Moon. Enter Champagne Charley. Enter the Monkey in clerical garb (female figure partly nude floating in the air beside him) fur cap coat with fur cuffs reading aloud a book of common prayer. Come Holy Ghost our souls inspire. Lightening flashing in the background. Enter old red man with red helmet on his head. Enter old bearded man in a high fur cap with closed eyes. Enter an Animal of No Importance. Enter a Virgin making much of time. Enter Renoir (female figure partly nude floating in the air beside him). If women had no breasts I would not have painted them. Enter H. D. wrapped in a palimpsest. Enter a welldressed man in every-day attire arm in arm with a Follies girl in a modish three-color one-piece club-striped combination travelo swimsuit. I've simply nothing to wear. Enter Prufrock in a Rock Fleece Overcoat. Enter Miss Everis. I am five months pregnant. The other day I felt a pain in my abdomen. Enter Steve Donoghue. Enter Kefalin winner of the Grand Prix. Enter an Onanist. Enter a Masochist. Enter Europe's Greatest Lover. Enter Antony and Cleopatra. Enter the Harvard Track Team. Enter Standard Oil Bearer right hand holding gloves left grasping staff of standard, so safe so sure so easy to handle. Enter Porphyria's Lover. Enter Mr. and Mrs. Lingam with an attendant behind. Enter a Jury of Annoyance. Enter Sportsman holding up a hare in his right hand. Enter a Feudal Ladye amorous to be known. Enter a Knight Errant. Enter T. noorder-quartier (halitoxio). Enter Nicolas Alfan de Ribera Marquis de Villanneva de las Torres de Dugnes d'Alcala Grands d'Espagne. Enter Lindberg with a Lion-Tamer. Enter Vandals and Visigoths. Enter the Pancake-Woman reading aloud What Every Girl Should Know. Enter Joseph telling his Dreams. Enter Blasus de Manfre, the Waterspouter. Enter Roman Youth Swallowing Stones (burst of applause from a London whore who appears standing between a lion and a unicorn). Enter an ignorant Physician. Enter a Fair Lady in Revolt. Enter Mr. Guy Holt with a flair for civilized fiction. Enter a Magician. Enter a Fawn dressed up as a Girl. Enter Queens in Hyacinth. Enter Jamaica God of Rum. Enter His Excellency Kno Sung Tao holding a jar (black idol) in both hands. Enter the Donkey Ambassador holding a lemon in both hands, very rare in this undivided state. Enter a Pederast holding a lip-stick in both hands. Enter John Paul Jones supported by an officer of the law white cravat hat and sword in right hand. Enter Marie Antoinette powdered hair lace silk combination pyjamas. Enter Shepherdesses pursued by Illustrious Americans. Enter Miss Atlantic Monthly. Brekete ex Kotex Kotex pursued by the Earl of Fitzdotterel's Eldest Son. I reflect with pleasure on the success with which the British undertakers have prospered this last summer. Enter the Ghost of Hamlet. Enter a Temple Boy. Enter Alpha and Omega. Enter the Soul killed by the Explosion. Enter Rimbaud. Enter Van Gogh. Enter Amon Ra. Enter the Star of the East. Enter the Stars. Enter the Youngest Princess. Enter the Queen of Peking. Enter the Moon. Enter Death stabbed in the Back. There is a Circle in the Centre. Enter the Grey Princess. Enter the Cramoisy Queen. Enter the Mad Queen. Enter the Sun.

The Blind Man leaves the scene, saying, I can see nothing.

THE SUN

When I look into the Sun I sun-lover sun-worshipper sun-seeker when I look into the Sun (sunne sonne soleil sol) what is it in the Sun I deify !

His Madness : his incorruptibility his central intensity and fire : his permanency of heat : his candle-power (fifteen hundred and seventy-five billions of billions 1,575,000,000,000,000,000,000,000,000) : his age and duration : his dangerousness to man as seen by the effects (heatstroke, isolation, thermic fever, siriasis) he sometimes produces upon the nervous system : the healing virtues of his rays (restores youthful vigor and vitality is the source of health and energy, oblivionizes ninety per cent of all human aches and pains) : his purity (he can penetrate into unclean places brothels privies prisons and not be polluted by them) : his magnitude (400 times as large as the moon) : his weight two octillions of tons or 746 times as heavy as the combined weights of all the planets) : his brilliance (5300 times brighter than the dazzling radiance of incandescent metal) : his distance from the earth as determined by the equation of light, the constant of abberation, the parallectic inequality of the moon (an aviator flying from the earth to the sun would require 175 years to make the journey) : his probable union in a single mass with the earth in the far-distant past : the probability that in some remote future he will begin to grow colder (there is a turning point in the life of every star) : his allotropic variations : his orbital motion : his course through the zodiac : his motion among the stars : his path along the ecliptic : his wingéd disk : his chariot : his diameter and dimensions : his depth and density, his rotation : his contraction : his daily appearance and disappearance : his image tattooed upon my back : his image formed in my mind : the colors of his spectrum as examined with special photographic plates, with a spectroheliograph, with an altazimuth, with a pyrheliometer, with an actionometer, with the bolometer, the radiomocrometer, the interferometer : his uninhabitability : the festivals held in his honor : the horses sacrificed in his honor : the obelisks dedicated in his honor : the verses recited in his honor : the dances danced by the Red Indians in his honor : the masks worn by the Aztecs in his honor : the self-torture endured by the Incas in his honor : his importance to the life of the earth, cut off his rays for even a single month and the earth would die : his importance to the life of the soul, cut off his rays for even a single hour and the soul would die : his disturbing influence on the motions of the moon : his attraction for Venus : his turbulence during a Transit of Venus : his contacts with Venus (internal and external) : his cosmical significance : his splendor and strength as symbolised by the seminal energy of the ox : his gold-fingered quietness in late Autumn : his whiteness in the Desert : his cold redness in Winter : his dark and sinister appearance before a Storm : his solid rotundity: his definiteness of form : his politeness in stopping for Joshua : his fascination for Icarus : his importance to the Ancient Mariner : his momentousness to the Prophet : his affiliation with Heliogabalus who married him to the moon : his mad influence over Aknaton : the reproductions of him by Van Gogh : the reproductions of him on old coins, on the American twenty-dollar gold piece, on the jackets of jockeys, on soap advertisements, in old woodcuts, on kindergarten blackboards, on the signs of old taverns : his tremendous influence on religions (among the Vedic Indians, among the Ancient Persians, among the Ancient Greeks, among the indigenous Americans, among the Ancient Romans, among the Babylonians and Assyrians, among the Ancient Egyptians, among the Hindoos among the Japanese) : the temples erected to his glory (in particular the great sun-temple of Baalbek) : his power of consuming souls : his unconcealed love for sun-dials (true as the dial to the sun) : the height he attains at the meridian: his family of asteroids : the occurrence of his name in ornithology, witness the sun-bittern (eurpyga helias) : among the vertebrates, witness the sun-fish or basking shark : in horticulture witness the tournesol, the heliotrope, the sunflower (helianthus annus) the marigold and the solsaece (from the word solsequium — sun-following) : his light — an uninterrupted continuance of gradation from the burning sunshine of a tropical noon to the pale luminosity that throws no shadow : his faculae and flocculi : his pederastic friendship with the Man in the Moon : the smallness of the target he offers to a meteorite (soul) arrowing toward him from infinity : the different behaviour of his spectral lines which are believed to originate at different levels and the relative Doppler displacements of the same spectral lines as given by his receding and advancing limbs : his importance in the Nebular Hypothesis: his personification in the form of a mirror in Japan: in the form of Ra in Egypt: his halos, rainbows and mirages : his eclipses, in particular the great Egyptian Eclipse of May 17 1882 : his nakedness : his red effrontery : his hot-tempered intolerance : his attraction for the earth (equal to the breaking strain of a steel rod three thousand miles in diameter) : his temperature (if he were to come as near as the moon, the solid earth would melt like wax) his reflection in the eyes of a girl (perihelion and aphelion) his mountains of flame which thrust upward into infinity: the fantastic shapes of his eruptive prominences (solar-lizards sun-dogs sharp crimson in color) : his brilliant spikes or jets, cyclones and geysers vertical filaments and columns of liquid flame: the cyclonic motion of his spots : his volcanic restlessness : his contortions: his velocity of three or four hundred miles an hour : his coronoidal discharges : his cyclonic protuberances, whirling fire spouts, fiery flames and furious commotions : his tunnel-shaped vortices : his equatorial acceleration : his telluric storms : his vibrations : his acrobatics among the clouds : his great display of sun-spots : his magnetic storms (during which the compass-needle is almost wild with excitement) : his prominences that have been seen to rise in a few minutes to elevations of two and three hundred thousand miles : his frenzy of turmoil : his periodic explosions : his madness in a lover's heart.

[*transition* 15, February 1929]

THE NEW WORD

- The New Word is the serpent who has sloughed off his old vocabulary.

The New Word is the stag who has rid himself of the old wood of his antlers.

The New Word is the clean piercing of a Sword through the rotten carcass of the Dictionary, the Dwarf standing on the shoulders of the Giant (Dictionary) who sees further into the Future than the giant himself, the Panther in the Jungle of Dictionary who pounces upon and devours all timid and facile words, the New Word is a Diamond Wind blowing out the Cobwebs of the Past.

The New Word is a direct stimulant upon the senses, a freshness of vision, an inner sensation, the egg from which other words shall be produced, a herald of revolt, the new tree thrusting above the dreary court-yard of No Change, a jewel upon the breast of Time, the Eve that stands naked before us, the challenge flung in the face of an unadventurous public, the reward of the discoverer, the companion of the prophet, the simplicity of the unexpected, the girder bridge towards a splendid future, the tremendous concentration and internal strength of a Joyce, the defiance of laws.

[*transition* 16–17, June 1929]

OBSERVATION-POST

A well-known phenomenon in the East is the False Dawn, a transient light on the horizon an hour before the True Dawn. The False Dawn = the poets sponsored by Amy Lowell and the Imagists who flickered for a brief instant on the horizon before they dwindled into the Robert Hillyers and Humbert Wolfs, the Edna Saint Vincent Millays, the Walter de la Mares, the Bénets and Untermeyers, the Auslanders and Teasdales who spot with their flytracks the bloated pages of our magazines and anthologies. Once again the general reader has been deceived by the False Dawn and has gone back to bed (who can blame him ?) thus missing the True Dawn which has definitely appeared on the horizon harbingered by T. S. Eliot, heralded by the Morning Star of Joyce and heliorayed with the bright shafts of Hart Crane, E. E. Cummings, Perse and MacLeish, Gertrude Stein, Desnos, Eluard, Jolas and Kay Boyle. It is regretable that Mr. Eastman should announce himself[1] as strongly opposed to this True Dawn which he regards as an affliction, regrettable because a man who can write a clear intelligent criticism (the average critic has much in common with a poor woman in Arabia — she will sell you milk if she has any) written without antagonism and in good taste, should never have made the mistake of confounding the wisdom of the True Dawn poets with madness. I recall Cocteau " the extreme limit of wisdom is what the public calls madness." ∴ Mr. Eastman = Public Opinion. And as Public Opinion despairs, so Mr. Eastman despairs because he finds Crane and Cummings and Joyce unfriendly. He feels they are uncommunicative. He begrudges the fact that they only incidentally allow one to look on not realizing the privilege of being allowed to look on with Crane or Cummings or Joyce (was it not a great privilege for

---

1. The Cult of Unintelligibility by Max Eastman, *Harper's Magazine*, April 1929.

the men of their times who were fortunate enough to look on with Keats or Shelley or Blake, and are these new men any less?) instead of having to grope among the mediocrities that darken the sky like a plague of locusts across the trajectory of the man who is arrowing himself into a New Splendor. And he bewails the poet who withdraws into himself, ignoring that the deeper the poet explores into the miracle of his own soul and his own flesh in quest of his Muse the stronger he will become, the more equipped to penetrate into the bridal chamber where his Muse waits for him white and naked and " lasciviously frail " —

> " i like my body when it is with your
> body. It is so quite a new thing.
> Muscles better and nerves more.
> i like your body. i like what it does,
> i like its hows. i like to feel the spine
> of your body and its bones, and the trembling
> — firm — smoothness and which I will
> again and again and again
> kiss, i like kissing this and that of you,
> i like, slowly stroking the, shocking fuzz
> of your electric furr, and what-is-it comes
> over parting flesh… And eyes big love-crumbs,
> and possibly I like the thrill
> of under me you so quite new."

This sonnet symbolizes the union of the Poet with his Muse. Result a Poem, not a pantalette poesy or a pastiche done up in petticoats, or a corseted whimper reeking of eau-de-cologne which is the union of the False Dawn poet with his stale and dowdy muse, but a Poem brutal and young and alive, sheer gold and barbaric, a Poem that stimulates the mind instead of coagulating it. For Cummings is always refreshing. He breaks laws and gives us what is new. He frees us from the stale confinement of the workshop. He brings us an erotic innocence. What he writes is for his own pleasure, hence his entire freedom from servitude. He writes of perpetual girls marching to love, of orchids whose velocity is sculptural, of a child's world that is puddle-wonderful, of the wind as a Lady with bright slender eyes, of young stars digging a grave with silver spades, of a girl naked amid unnaked things, of locomotives and roses. He begins a sonnet

" after all white horses are in bed."

He ends another

" but if I like, i'll take between thy hands
what no man feels, no woman understands."

He writes a love-poem (almost all his poems are love-poems) *Puella Mea* that rivals Villon, he writes a novel *The Enormous Room* which is, after *Ulysses*, the most important novel written since the War, he writes a play *Him* which has no parallel either in France (exception made for *Orphée*) or in America. Yet Mr. Eastman deplores Cummings, he thinks that Cummings' poetry should be *seen* because it is composed so largely of punctuation that it cannot be heard (an entirely erroneous impression) and that Cummings' use of the comma, or is it the semicolon, is deplorable. I am afraid Mr. Eastman runs the danger of being what Robert Sage would call a " comfortable critic " — " Comfortable critics betray themselves outrageously when they estimate E. E. Cummings merely as an outspoken young man who puts a semicolon in the centre of a word and begins a line with a comma."

However it is on such topics (punctuation and alphabetical freedom) that Mr. Eastman, in spite of his intentional sarcasm, is most interesting. He suggests that there are other freedoms to be won. " Why should the letters within a word be permitted to congregate forever in the same dull, old, conventional and sleepy groups ? " and the answer is why indeed ? Joyce, Cummings,

Gillespie, Jolas have cracked open words as a roadmender cracks stone, for a NEW ROAD. By doing this they have destroyed Philistine conceptions of law and servitude, they have brought about a disintegration of words, and they have dynamited the language into a new and reinvigorated structure.

Mr. Eastman offers us another suggestion still couched in an ironic vein : " Why not a little spontaneity of arrangement and the occasional eruption of an Arabic or Chinese or Russian letter[2] that happens to linger in the memory and chime with the whims of the poet ? Or a poet might abandon the alphabet altogether and make a new one more congenial to his inner life." Tant mieux ! I say *anything* as long as it shatters to pieces the mocking mirrors of hypocrisy and the cheap vases stuffed with the attrape-poussiere flowers of banality.

Frost, Sandburg, Masters, A. E. Housman, Yeats, the Comtesse de Noailles, even Valéry (exception made for his Cimetière Marin) are not False Dawn poets but neither are they poets of the True Dawn because they are not nor ever were *in advance*. They never believed with Rimbaud and the poets of the True Dawn that the inventions of the unknown demand new forms. They remain dromedaries with the power to race but unfortunately muzzled with the halter of the past.

Mr Eastman continues " A little cross-breeding between plus signs and semicolons would be a good beginning. By crossing the minus sign with the colon we got the sign of division ; a cross between a plus sign and a semicolon might give us something more remarkable. " *Yes* why not (I refer Mr Eastman to the Gillespie essays in *transition*) for the list of drinks must be altogetherabsolutelyentirely changed, a new barman substituted, and all the belly-wash concoctions of the milk-and-water-weak-tea-orangeade-lemon-squash-gingerale-sarsparilla-root-beer-ice-

2. Mr. Eastman might be interested in the current number of *Les Cahiers d'Art* where there is a documentary study of the symbols for words used by the natives of the Easter Islands.

cream-soda variety abolished in favor of Red Heart Rum, Double Stingers and Irish Whiskey. I drink to Kay Boyle

> " Of days spread like peacock tails
> Of days worn savagely like parrot-feathers."

No whimperings here, no growing pains, no hospital poems, no red skeletons, no condescensions, no nambypamby mollycoddle apron-string vinal-veranda-verse. This is Kay Boyle hard and glorious and defiant, this is Kay Boyle and nobody but Kay Boyle.

I drink to Theo Rutra the young Czecho-Slovakian poet whose poem is the cool tinkling of ice in a tall glass of gin.

> " The loorbalboli glides through the algroves suddenly turning upon itself. There is a spiral spatter of silver. A thunderbelt lies in white. The rolls drum down the hidden malvines, where the gullinghales flap finwings casually. The feathers of the salibri glint in the marlite. Then the loorabalboli sings : 'O puppets of the eremites, the weed-maids fever love. Send Octobus to shores of clay; thieve younglings out of sheaves of ice.' And troutroots dance. There is a blish. A wonderlope whirs through the floom."

I drink to MacLeish who shares with Perse the qualities of timelessness, of self-control, of seriousness, of a perfect sense of equilibrium, of the analogy between life and the progress of the soul.

> "Be proud New York of your prize docks
> And your doors and the size of your trains and your dancing
> Elegant big clean girls and your
> Niggers with narrow heels and the blue on their
> Bad mouths and your automobiles in the
> Struck steel light and your jews
> And your bright boys and your sorrowsweet singing

> Tones and your signs wincing out in the wet
> Cool shine and the twinges of
> Green against evening…
>
>   When the towns go down there are stains of
> Rust on the stone shores and illegible
> Coins and a rhyme remembered of
>   swans say
> Or birds or leaves or a horse or fabulous
> Bull forms or a falling of gold upon
> Softness
>
>   Be proud City of Glass of your
> Brass roofs and the bright peaks of your
> Houses. Town that stood to your knees in the
> Sea water, be proud, be proud
> Of your high gleam on the sea
>   But who
> Town will marry your name to the name of a
> Talking beast that the place of your walls be remembered ?"[3]

I drink from a bottle of Cutty Sark to Hart Crane — sailors hurricanes comets and a diamond wind to blow out the sick fogs of the brain. He is dynamic energy, concentration, fresh vision, a migratory crane flying above the worn-out forest of the poetic phrase, above the false and stagnant pools of artificiality. He has for ancestors Marlowe and Coleridge and Whitman and Rimbaud —

O CARIB ISLE ;

> The tarantula rattling at the lily's foot,
> across the feet of the dead, laid in white sand

---

[3]. No commas here for Mr. Eastman to worry about.

near the coral beach, — the small and ruddy crabs
flickering out of sight, that reverse your name ; —

and above, the lyric palsy of eucalypti, seeping
a silver swash of something unvisited... Suppose
I count these clean, enamel frames of death,
brutal necklaces of shells around each grave
laid out so carefully. This pity can be told...

And in the white sand I can find a name, albeit
in another tongue. Tree-name, flower-name deliberate,
gainsay the unknown death... The wind
sweeping the scrub palms, also is most kind.

But who is the Captain of this doubloon isle
without a turnstile ? Nought but catchword crabs
vining the hot groins of the underbrush ? Who
the Commissioner of mildew throughout the senses ?
His Carib mathematics dull the bright new lenses.

Under the poinciana, of a noon or afternoon
let fiery blossoms clot the light, render my ghost,
sieved upward, black and white along the air —
until it meets the blue's comedian host.

Let not the pilgrim see himself again
bound like the dozen turtles on the wharf
each twilight, — still undead, and brine caked in their eyes,
huge, overturned : such thunder in their strain !
And clenched beaks coughing for the surge again !

Slagged of the hurricane, — I, cast within its flow,
congeal by afternoons here, satin and vacant...

> You have given me the shell, Satan, — the ember,
> Carbolic, of the sun exploded in the sea.

Yet Mr Eastman includes Hart Crane among his Unintelligibles. No doubt he is afraid of Hurricranes.

Let us now pour Irish Whiskey into our glasses and begin by agreeing with Mr Eastman about James Joyce: that Joyce not only polishes the words which he sets in a row but moulds them and fires them in his own oven ; that from free grammar Joyce, who is equipped for creative etymology as few men ever were, has taken a further step to free etymology ; that Joyce has a prodigiously fine ear and a fine sense of humor. But when Mr. Eastman contends that Joyce speaks a private language whose meaning cannot be conveyed to the reader, when he contends that the literary form of Joyce's *Work in Progress*[4] finds its parallel in the madhouse, and when he contends that the only thing the reader can experience with Joyce is a kind of elementary tongue dance, I cry NO. The fact that a Stuart Gilbert, a Rodker, a McAlmon, a MacLeish, a Jolas can follow with intense pleasure the footprints of Joyce's brain along the path of the ecliptic through the thunderclap, beyond the marriage according to auspices, beyond the burial of the dead, into a divine providence (I refer to the four cardinal points of the book) is sufficient justification, if a justification were necessary, of this Work and of its Sanity. Are there as many men can follow Einstein ? But because only a handful can follow him should this detract one iota from his achievement ? Ask not the Eagle to descend to the crow but let us train ourselves to become eagles. Let us spread new wings as if for flight.

In America there seems to be a deeply rooted hatred against the creator for altering the rules of the game (as the game in the

---

4. Book I appeared in *transition* issues 1 to 8 inclusive. *transition* number 11 contained a fragment of Book II ; and Book III has appeared in *transition* numbers 12, 13, and 15.

case of a real poet is always played on his home ground we should conform to his rules) a blaming of the author if they cannot understand him (did they ever consider blaming themselves for this fault ?) and an entire lack of sympathy with whatever does not come curtsey-curtseying to them. And what is this absolute necessity for understanding ? Isn't it enough that a book or a painting awake response rather than meaning ? Can one always understand Picasso ? Does his work have to be stifled with the haberdashery of understanding ? I prefer his paintings hard and naked. I invite Mr Eastman and those who are interested in the reading of Joyce to study Robert McAlmon's enlightening essay on the *Work in Progress*[5] where he says " it is natural that a literature should emerge which is evocative rather than explanatory, more intent upon composite types, plots, and situations, than on particularized meanings. " Cannot music be appreciated without the necessity of being understood ? Does one have to understand a beautiful woman or the stars in order to love them ?

Joyce is the Great Alchemist of the Word, the Paracelsus of Prose, the Transmuter of metal words into words of gold. He invents the word ' auriscenting ' (to catch the smell of something on the breeze) ; he coins the new word ' cropulence ' a combination of corpulence and crapulence ; he takes the vowels out of the word ' thunderclap ' and gives us ' thyndwrclxpz ' ; he removes the letter ' g ' from the word ' strength ' when he wishes to show the dying out of desire like the dying out of the colors of a rainbow ; he refers to the days of the week as moanday, tearsday, wailsday, thumpsetay, frightday, shatterday, Sear of the Law ; he speaks of faith hope and charity as fakes hoax and carrotty ; he refers to Shaw as Pshaw ; to Wyndham Lewis' *Time and Western Man* as *Spice and Westend Woman* (" utterly exhausted before publication ") ; to Benjamin Franklin as Benjermine Funkling because ' funkel ' in German means electric spark and Franklin is the American Prometheus ;

---

5. *Mr. Joyce Directs An Irish Prose-Ballet* by Robert McAlmon *transition 15.*

he describes Tristan coming back in armour as coming back in a 'chemise de fer'; when he wishes to say mum's the word he uses the Latin aqua in buccat (keep water in your mouth); he refers to Anna Livia Plurabella, as analytical plausible, as Annushka Lutetiavitch Pufflovah, as Amnis Limina Permanent, as Auld Letty Plussiboots; he compares the smoking of a domestic cocoa-pot to Popocatepetl; when he uses the word 'kicksheets' he is thinking of Shakespeare's Doll Tearsheets; he writes ichabod, habakuk, opanoff, uggamyg, hapaxle, gomenon, ppppfff to describe the gutteral and inarticulate sounds of peasants engaged in amatory struggles in the dark, and he ironically uses a long scientific word (nichtsnichtsundnichts) for an insect because he wants a word longer than the insect itself; he gives us the clue to a long and complicated sentence (it took Joyce three days to write this sentence) by using the word 'finish' at the end to show that the words are of Finnish derivation; in the passage of The Triangle he compares one brother (Shaun) to Arithmetic and the other brother (Shem) to Algebra and then uses words of Arab derivation because the Arabs were the inventors of Algebra. Woven into the tale of Anna Livia Pluribelle[6] are the names of more than five hundred rivers and in the fable of The Ondt and the Gracehoper[7] there are perhaps as many names for insects. He speaks of playing " hopptociel bommptaterre ;" he parodies his own verse in Chamber-Music " adieu adroit adieu atout atous "; he feeds us a clean provender of words : hourihaleine, unuchorn, revermer, bannistars, engauzements ; he creates the sound of thunder " Mattahah ! Marahah ! Luahah ! Joahanahanahana "; and he can be as slender and frail as the miracle of the crescent moon. I quote from the Mookse and The Gripes[8], the passage about Nuvoletta who is a little cloud over the Vatican.

---

6. *Anna Livia Plurabelle* by James Joyce, New York, Crosby Gaige, 1928.
7. *Three Fragments from Work in Progress* by James Joyce, Paris, Black Sun Press, 1929.
8. As above.

" Nuvoletta in her lightdress, spunn of sisteen shimmers was looking down on them, leaning over the bannistars and listening all she childishly could. She was alone. All her nubied companions were asleeping with the squirrels...
She tried all the winsome wonsome ways her four winds had taught her. She tossed her sfumastelliacinous hair like *la princesse de la Petite Bretagne* and she rounded her mignons arms like Mrs. Cornwallis-West and she smiled over herself like the beauty of the image of the post of the daughter of the queen of the Emperour of Irelande and she sighed after herself as were she born to bride with Tristis Tristior Tristissimus...
O, how it was dusk! From Vallée Maraia to grasyaplaina, dormimost Echo! Ah dew! Ah dew! It was so dusk that the tears of night began to fall, first by ones and twos, then by threes and fours, at last by fives and sixes of sevens, for the tired ones were wecking, as we weep now with them. O! O! O! Par la pluie !...
The Nuvoletta reflected for the last time in her little long life and she made up all her myriads of drifting minds in one. She cancelled all her engauzements. She climbed over the bannistars; she gave a childy cloudy cry : *Nuée ! Nuée !* A lightdress fluttered. She was gone... "

Is this the cult of the unintelligible? Is this a literature of the madhouse? I think that Mr Eastman will agree with me that it is not and that this is as pure poetry as man has ever been privileged to read. But whatever he or the public agree or do not agree upon is of small consequence to those who believe as I do that Joyce is the Central Luminary of Modern Literature around which revolve the Fiery Comets of the True Dawn.

[*transition* 16–17, June 1929]

DREAMS 1928–1929

La Pureté du rêve, l'inemployable, l'inutile du rêve, voilà ce qu'il s'agit de défendre contre une nouvelle rage de ronds-de-cuir qui va se déchainer.
　　ARAGON: *Traité du Style.*

1

the dream of the glass princess is a cool moonlight of glass wings each wing a beat of the heart to greet the glass princess she is not bigger than a thimble as she tiptoes daintily down the tall glass corridor of my soul tinkle by tinkle tinkle by tinkle until I feel I shall go mad with suspense but just as she is opening her mouth to speak there is a shattering of glass and I awake to find I have knocked over the pitcher of ice-water that in summer always stands like a cold sentinel on the red table by the bed

2

red funnels are vomiting tall smokeplumes gold and onyx and diamond and emerald into four high round circles which solidify before they collide together with the impact of billiard balls that soon are caromed by a thin cue of wind into the deep pockets of sleep

3

the Man in the Moon is as rose-colored as our finger-nails as we go out hand in hand into the garden you and I to somewhere beyond the sleeping roses but although you remove your silk stockings and I my silk socks (we have forgotten our calling cards) the star butler with his silver tray never reappears and we are forced to find our way home along the bottom of the lake

4

I am rattling dice in a yellow skull they are falling upon the floor at the feet of the plump woman with bare breasts who is absorbed in the passion of giving milk to a rattlesnake but as soon as the numbers on the face of the dice correspond to the number of birds of paradise that form the jewels of her necklace she withdraws behind a red counterpane for the purpose of concealment

5

a naked lady in a yellow hat

6

I am a lean Siamese cat who insists upon sleeping under the bed in order to watch the mouse-holes so I am not particularly astonished when I wake up next morning to find myself under the bed

7

there is a tree too high for me to reach its top until the young girl with the blonde hair and the white white skin (she wears furs and a veil) proposes that we take flying lessons whereupon I climb to the top of the tree and set at liberty my soul but when I slide down again to the ground the girl is disappearing out of sight on a tricycle and I am powerless to climb back again

8

they the twelve lions prowl swiftly out of a long iron tunnel and the entire dream is a waiting to be torn in pieces

9

I begin to take it as a matter of course that no girl under ten years of age can in any circumstances swim more than a given number of strokes and naturally when the whole question has become one of formula I am not surprised when these girls look up at me and drown without more than a perfunctory show of resistance

10

a horse dealer is looking into a horse's mouth and examining its teeth but I am far more interested in the young cripple who holds up a wax leg for me to light as I would light a candle and by the light of his flaming leg I am able to read the book of one hundred ways of kissing girls which he has been able to buy with the profits he has obtained by the selling of his large stock of artificial eyes

11

P S the maid never returned to turn down the bed each word illuminated in a different color but all the other pages of the letter (my fingers inform me that there are a great many of them) are as blank as the ceiling of my bedroom white as the linen sheets except for that strange last page P S the maid never returned to turn down the bed nor can I find out the author of this letter (the writing suggests the influence of the rainbow) nor can I ever know what bed is referred to (there have been so many beds) nor who the maid is who never chooses to return

12

    I do not find it strange that a blue bird should fall in love with a playing card because the playing card in question happens to be the queen of hearts

13

    I am in a girl's soul (as we all live and sleep in a certain sense in our beloved's soul) among the frail crumpled garments of her thought cast here and there in disarray by invisible hands (are they hers are they mine or are they perhaps the ardent hands of time) the fallen petals of her apparel symbolic of her former vagaries, the dress discarded on the floor of her imagination the discarded robe of her past, her red slippers petulantly kicked into a corner of her brain like a pair of red-throated scruples, the broken girdle at her waist for a sign of desire, slender ribbons to suggest slender nights of love slenderer than rainbows at dawn, while all her hair becomes a mysterious undercurrent flowing through me (the new blood flowing through my arteries) but the pleasantest part of this dream is the awakening at the blue hour before the dawn to find her sleeping at my side

14

    battleships emerge painted grey and black (they are lean as arrows) a submarine comes to the surface flying the skull and crossbones red icebergs drift like tombs upon the waves — with a red sword I trace upon the great whalelike back of the submarine the red words of war she spurts a jet of fire and sinks below the surface while I race over the horizon in pursuit of the mad dryad widespread upon a dolphin but as I am catching up to her there is a knock on my door and the femme de chambre announces il est sept heures monsieur

15

    a nightmare in the shape of an empty bed in the centre of a tall room upon the bed lies one of those long pistols the kind formerly used in dueling I am kneeling on one side of the bed my uncle is kneeling on the other side the horror of the dream being who will first dare to reach for the revolver the strain being so great that I am exhausted all the next day although this nightmare has repeated itself more than once

16

    it is night one infinitesimal grain of sand swells and swells and swells and swells until it is an enormous circular beach which suddenly tilts and slides down into the sea leaving me clinging to the handle of a large red umbrella which is automatically opening and shutting against a windy sky (I notice the stars have all been blown away) but nothing more happens till I feel in my ears the insistent burring of an alarm clock

17

    a giraffe is gorging himself on sunflowers a Parisian doll is washing herself in a blue fingerbowl while I insist on their electrocution on the grounds of indecency

18

    the Ritz Tower sways like a drunkard under the cold fire of the moon while the Botticelli chorus girl is busily cutting her toe nails to the great astonishment of a bottle of gin which stares out at her from behind a pair of white tennis shoes

19

I am endeavoring to pursuade a Chinese professor who is at work on a torpedo which he expects to shoot to the sun to allow me to live in the centre of this torpedo

20

the dream of the sporting scene consists of three clowns (no doubt the Fratellini) lying behind coverts formed by bushes one of the clowns is about to shoot a tiger which is ravenously devouring a tethered tight rope walker who has been used as a decoy the unpleasant part of this dream being that I am the tiger

21

all night I dream I am an eagle winging over deserts of insanity in pursuit of the drunken birds of her eyes but although this has been a recurring dream I have never succeeded in catching both birds in the same night one night it is the left eye on another the right eye but last night for the first time (let this be a good omen) the eagle overtook and devoured both of the birds at once and this morning I have the sensation of a complete virginity of victory

22

a black and yellow bird morbidly tender with a feminine name excites, by her musical exercises, one of a Jewish sect who lies on a portable bed. Among a thicket of red windflowers, but, in spite of his entreaties, she is unyielding, and he is forced to resume his relations (lascivious) with a corpulent Spanish Lady the back of whose neck I have marked with my teeth, much to the consternation of a young Miss Eraser who, until now, had labored under the delusion that everything could be removed by rubbing

23

Behind a painting of the Virgin with child — a sudden appearing and disappearing of the Nightgown!

[*transition* 18, November 1929]

FOR A PROTECTION

I see part of her face part of her mouth moving in salutation making amends for the light wind that unravels her hair. I realize that the Turkish doll I am bringing to her for a plaything is inadequate. There is for background a Greek colonnade a mere incident in the measure of the dream which is brought to a close by her turning into a heavy silk fabric which I wind around me as a protection against the antarctic cold which no doubt made itself felt in my dream because all my bedclothes had fallen off during the night.

[*transition* 18, November 1929]

ILLUSTRATIONS OF MADNESS

1

As boys raise a kite in the air so there is lifted into my brain the word Explosion which explodes and explodes in the intellect for hours at a time, and no matter how much I wish to direct my mind to other objects and banish the explosions, I find myself unable to do so because the word keeps exploding in my mind to the exclusion of all other thoughts. I am during the entire time aware that the explosion is subconscious and does not belong to the train of my own cogitations.

2

I can cause good sense to appear as insanity, distort the wisest institutions of civilized society into the practices of barbarians and strain Christianity into a jest book.

3

My heart is a madhouse for the twin lunatics of her eyes.

4

I rejoice in that dangerous automatic liberty which deprives man of the volition which constitutes him a being responsible for his actions.

5

I continually feel hurricanes of magic storming into me as wild and insane as eagles catapulting themselves into the sun.

6

I have heard for days and nights on end the reverberation crashing in my head of all the skyscrapers and buildings of the world, the reverberation of the crashing of ships in the fog at sea, the reverberation of the crashing of iron thoughts on the cold floor of the brain.

7

There is in me the infernal fury of the Sun by means of which I practice atrocities on the philistines. The operation of my fury is instantaneous and I abandon them to the malignity of my scorn and ridicule.

8

All compromise with me is impossible.

9

The inward nerves of my vision are beyond the sentiments of my heart and have no communication with the operations of my intellect. I boast of having effected this in a very complete manner by having caught and distilled certain rays of light from the Sun.

10

Because of a machine of light in my brain, because of the interposition of a wall of words (amor fire velocity invulnerability), because of the spells and incantations of a Sorceress I am beyond the force of assailment. In order to ascertain whether this be true or not let them decapitate me. They will find a hollow shell where once the Arrow burned. It will have gone to RĀ.

[*transition* 18, November 1929]

SHORT INTRODUCTION TO THE WORD

1)

Take the word Sun which burns permanently in my brain. It has accuracy and alacrity. It is monomaniac in its intensity. It is a continual flash of insight. It is the marriage of Invulnerability with Yes, of the Red Wolf with the Gold Bumblebee, of Madness with Rā

2)

Birdileaves, Goldabbits, Fingertoes, Auroramor, Barbarifire, Parabolaw, Peaglecock, Lovegown, Nombrilomane

3)

I understand certain words to be single and by themselves and deriving from no other words as for instance the word I

4)

I believe that certain physical changes in the brain result in a given word — this word having the distinguished characteristic of unreality being born neither as a result of conotation nor of conscious endeavor : Starlash

5)

There is the automatic word as for instance with me the word Sorceress; when the word goes on even while my attention is focused on entirely different subjects just as in swimming my arms and legs go on automatically even when my attention is focused on subjects entirely different from swimming such as witchcraft for instance or the Sorceress

6)

A nursery game called Hunt-the-Slipper. A flower called Lady-Slipper. Running in the Gold Cup a horse called Slipper. Drinking champagne out of Her Red Slipper. From these magic sources the development of the word Slipper in my mind so that it becomes the word internal and therefore as much a part of me as my eyes or feet.

7)

Honorificabilitudinity, Incircunscriptibleness, Antidisestablishment-Arians.

8)

The evolution of a word in the mind requires despotic power and unlimited elimination. How could Yes for instance flourish among words such as dog or corset or safety-pin or hot-water-bag or eunuch.

[*transition* 18, November 1929]

SLEEPING TOGETHER

these dreams for Caresse
"fermons les yeux pour voir"

FOR A PROTECTION

I see part of your face part of your mouth moving in salutation making amends for the light wind that unravels your hair. I realize that the snowball I am bringing to you for a plaything is inadequate. There is for background a white colonnade a mere incident in the measure of the dream which is brought to a close by your turning into a heavy silk fabric which I wind around me as a protection against the cold wind which no doubt made itself felt in my dream because all our bedclothes had fallen off during the night.

WHITE SLIPPER

A white aeroplane whiter than the word Yes falls like a slipper from the sky. You come dancing over the silver thorns of the lawn and by holding up the corners of your rose-and-white skirt you catch the white slipper which I kick down to you from the sun.

WHITE CLOVER

There is a clairvoyance of white clover, a coming towards me of the white star-fish of your feet, an aeolus of drapery. Your hand on the knob of the door is the timidity of the new moon, your hair over your shoulders a cataract of unloosened stars, your slender arms the white sails you lift to the mast of my neck. Not even the silkiness of newdrawn milk can compare to your skin, not even the cool curves of amphora can compare to the cool curves of your breasts, not even the epithalamiumic gestures of an Iseult can compare to your queenliness. Your ears are the littlest birds for the arrows of my voice, your lap the innocent resting place for the hands of my desire. And as you sit nude and shy on the edge of our bed I wonder at the miracle of the opening of your eyes.

SAFETY-PIN

Audaciously you put on the hat belonging to the lady and walk with me down the abrupt declivity to the sea. A large body of water confronts us whereon is no ship wherein is no fish (so we are told by the skeleton of the fisherman) so that we are spared the anxiety of sharks. You are preparing to undress and are taking off your rings preparatory to putting them in the conch-shell which I hold up to you. You are having difficulties with a safety-pin while I remain an appreciative spectator. We are interrupted by the four winds whistling together over the burial of the dead but though we searched up and down the beach we found no corpse and we were forced or rather you were forced to return to the problem of the safety-pin which refused to open for the simple reason that your fingers were inadequate to the occasion.

HUMAN FLESH AND GOLDEN APPLES

Like the horses of Diomedes I am being nourished with human flesh while you are eating the golden apples of the Hesperides. I suppose they are the apples of the Hesperides for they are so very big and gold. There is a clean sound of gravel being raked. The shadows under your eyes are blue as incense. Your voice is the distant crying of night-birds, your body is the long white neck of the peacock as she comes down the gravel path. Your mouth is an acre of desire so much as may be kissed in a day, our love the putting together of parts of an equation, so that when they knocked on the door at nine o'clock I could not believe that you were in the country and I alone in a hotel in New York forced to take consolation in the bottle of white rum that I bought last night from the elevator boy.

I BREAK WITH THE PAST

In a hot office building a man is dictating a letter to a bright-eyed stenographer who has just graduated from the College of Progress. Dear Madam I regret to inform you that your swans have sleeping sickness, but I am far away in the country wandering across the golf links your bright-colored scarf around my neck. I cannot seem to find you. I look into every bunker. I ask the caddy with the gluttonous face. I call out loud to the birds. I keep remembering how good-looking you are with your bedroom eyes and your new-moon ears. I begin to run. It is growing late for the red wolf of the sun has almost disappeared into his cavern of night. I run over the wooden bridge. I break with the past and race into the future over the far end of the links feeling myself fly through the air towards two sensations of light which turn out to be your eyes. When I wake up I am as tired as a marathon runner.

GOLDEN SPOON

Your body is the golden spoon by means of which I eat your soul. I do not seek to find the explanation for this curious sensation which is more visual than tactile. But I am afraid of the army of silver spoons marshaled in array under their commander-in-chief Silver Fork who is about to give the command to march against the golden spoon which I hold desperately in my mouth.

AUNT AGATHA

A leg should be more than a leg you said and I agreed. There are caterpillars underfoot you said and I agreed for I could feel my bare feet squashing a liquid something. The secret of love is to be animalistic you said and I agreed for I like panthers. But when you said let us go to call on Aunt Agatha I tied you face downward across a chair, turned up your clothes with the utmost precision and was just on the point of lashing you with a silver switch when there was a shriek of laughter as the Gay Duchess and Elsa de Brabent burst into the room to tell us that their niece Little Lady Lightfoot had been expelled from school for havinf been caught in the act of kissing the Yellow Dwarf. Here the dream ended for I felt you pressing knowingly into my arms and I realized that it must be long after seven to judge by the position of the sun as reflected in the twin mirrors of your eyes.

IT IS SNOWING

We are preparing ourselves for the horrors of war by viewing an autopsy. A trained nurse depressingly capable sits by a stove reading aloud from the Madonna of the Sleeping Cars while you insist on telling me that for three years the chorus girls have not come to Touggourt. There is a turmoil of passionate red except for my hands which are two drifts of white snow lying upon the cool shells of your breasts. It is snowing and there are people in galoshes and when we wake up it is snowing and there is the sound of the men shovelling the snow off the sidewalks. It is one of those cold grey days when the wise thing for us to do is to go to sleep again like bears in the wintertime.

WHITE AEROPLANES IN FLIGHT

We are flying. Below us the land is a sheet of notepaper scrawled over by the words of roads and rivers. A cemetery is a game of chess. A ploughed field is an accordeon. Black hayricks are crows. We are one of an astonishing pack of white aeroplanes a million million in number filling the sky with a myriad white points of light hunting after the red fox of the sun. We lose him among the clouds. We find him again. But he eludes us and burrows out of sight into the blue tunnel of the sea and you and I are confronted by the unpleasant problem of having to alight in the Place Vendome because we must cash a cheque at the bank before we can take a room at the Ritz. We awake to a bang. It is the femme de chambre closing the windows of our room while Narcisse is barking to be let out.

MIRACULOUS MESSAGE

I am in a parlor car. I am in a dining car. I am in a sleeping car. I have the upper berth so that I cannot look out the window but I have the apprehensive feeling of things happening in the dark outside. A bearded creature carrying a telegram in his mouth as a dog often carries a newspaper is trying to get on the train. I know in advance it is for me believing what I cannot prove. I feel that I am indivisible with the telegram but I am not able to put my hand through the steel side of the car. I have already decided to hide it under the roof of my tongue when I am sleepily aware of a body stirring in my arms and of the utter uselessness of the telegram which could not possibly contain such a miraculous message as your " Are you awake Dear."

EMBRACE ME YOU SAID

Embrace me you said but my arms were riveted to the most exacting of walls, embrace me you said but my mouth was sealed with the huge hot fruit of red wax, embrace me you said but my eyes were seared by the severities of two thousand winters — embrace me you said in such a low and feline voice that my eyes began to open like frightened shutters, in such a low and feline voice that my mouth became unsealed like red ice in a bowl of fire, in such a low and feline voice that my chains dropped like silver needles to the floor and my arms were free to encircle the white satin nudity of your voice which I tore into thin strips of music to store away in my heart whose desert had been threatened with vast armies of female laborers marching down dusty roads strewn with the prickly leaves of the cactus plant.

A PROGRESS UPWARD

Occuring at rare intervals is a dream of fairy-tale lightness more swift than the flight of tennis-balls. This dream consists of a progress upward towards a light metallic fire (sweet-smelling as a sun-ray) which pours like honey into a minute orifice rigidly exact whose organ of hearing is adjusted to the harmony of your hands.

WHITE FIRE

Your throat in my dream is a sensation of light so bright so sudden that I am dominated by the image of white fire far beyond the moment of ordinary awakening.

REVIRGINATE

A swift metallic monster with eyes more precious than diamonds rich in the secrets of sun and wind whirs with the whizzing sound of an arrow into the direct centre of my dream from which you turn sleepily with what *is* the matter what *is* the matter until we both fall asleep again under your grey squirrel coat which I pull over our heads for it is bitter cold.

ANIMAL MAGNETISM

All the sailors are laughing. It is contagious. All the whores are yawning. It is contagious. And all night long we wear ourselves out trying to laugh and yawn at one and the same time.

[*transition* 19–20, June 1930]

POEMS FROM THE DECACHORD,
BLUES, THE MORADA, PAGANY, AND
FOUR ANTHOLOGIES

photo of Harry Crosby

OUR LADY OF TEARS.

   She stood in Rama where the voice was heard
   Of Rachel sobbing by a barren bed :
   She watched the sword of Herod flashing red
In Bethlehem when in and out it erred
Among the innocents. And, undeterred,
   She summons vanished faces from the dead ;
   She wears a diadem upon her head,
and floats among the sleepless like a bird.

And who is there in the unjoyous world
   Who has not broken bread with her, or known
The melancholy sadness of her sighs,
Or felt a muffled darkness as she curled
   In snaky arabesques as cold as stone
Within the bitter heart she crucifies ?

[*The Decachord*, Vol. IV, No. 15, March–April 1928]

BILITIS

Showers of silver rain and rose-grey dawn,
   And afterwards fierce sunny-golden heat,
   Pretext for Bilitis to turn her feet
To where a forest dreams beyond the lawn.

Naked she strays, shy, gracile as a fawn,
   All virginal and innocent and sweet,
   Queen of the woodland solitude of Crete,
And lovely as a goddess heaven-born.

Ungarmented, a favourite tree she climbs,
   Bare knees pressed close, upweaving through the dark,
Until astride a thrusting bough, widespread,
She, clinging, swings her legs in space, and rhymes
Her cadence to the branches overhead,
   And feels the dryad's kiss beneath the bark.

[*The Decachord*, Vol. V, No. 20, November–December 1929]

TRUMPET OF DEPARTURE

> (and the ships shall be
> broken all they that are not able to go
> to the sun)

Abominable dead harbor of the Past. You are the poison Satan urges me to drink. I smell the stench of your wharves even to this day. Your coils of rope are serpents ready to strike. Your warehouses house enormous sacks of bric a brac (ha ! the tyranny of things). Your tumbrel-wagons are piled high with the empty barrels of hypocrisy. Your tug-boats ferry-boats swan-boats pleasure-boats dredger-boats were never destined to venture out into the storms of the sea. Your customs officers have never handled ingots of gold from the quarries of the sun. Your freight cars have never rattled off across the country with a cargo of naked slave girls. Your lighthouse is a false prophet.

I see your schoolhouse threatening my innocence with false values. I see your church on the wharf standing like a fisherman with baited hook to catch my soul. I see your brothel staring with empty window-eyes a door wide open for mouth. O see your tavern-bar. It contains a thousand bottles and a thousand hells. I see your men and women hyenas with the snarl of fear branded upon their faces. I hear the sound of their quarrelling.

To do something to escape this evil. To kindle a flame within the walls of the heart. To seek a boon on high.

I put on habiliments of war. I hoist sail. I set the flag of madness on the tallest mast. I sound the trumpet of departure. I unanchor the past.

The word Fire is the secret of the opening of the harbor gates.

The harbor lights dwindle behind me.

There is the clean wind of the sea. I become clean as an arrow in flight. I burn into the wind. I catapult through tunnels of delirium into a hurricane of stars. There is a thunder of drums a blare of trumpets a crescendo of Sun.

[*Blues,* Vol. I, No. 5, 1929]

SCORN

you business men with your large desks, with your stenographers and your bell-boys and your private telephones, I say to you these are the four walls of your cage.

you are tame as canaries with your small bird-brains where lurks the evil worm, you are fat from being over-fed, you know not the lean wild sunbirds that arrow down paths of fire.

I despise you, I am too hard to pity you, I would hang you on the gallows of the Stock Exchange, I would flay you with taxes, I would burn you alive with the wall Street Journals, I would condemn you to an endless round of bank banquets, I deride you I mock at you I laugh you to scorn.

[*The Morada* 1, Fall 1929]

DESOLATE

the coast is desolate and
    encrusted with salt
the sea has encroached
    far on the land
naked crags
lift themselves from a sea of grey
worn and denuded stumps
    of mountains
standing for untold ages
    above the sea
their shoulders are
lifted high above the
    tree line
      their summits stand
      out gaunt and lonely
      in an unbroken solitude

the season is one of rain
and the old ruined castle
    stands in isolation
the blackening of the walls
    from the smoke of the hearth
the rain-water from the
    roof collecting in the gutters
these are the symbols
    for my loneliness

when you have gone

[*The Morada* 2, Winter 1930]

103°

What is this feverish plucking of the sheets these horizons of fire these thunder-girls with eyes of lightning who come carronnading down the hot cylinders of my brain. They come to torture me with thirst they squeeze clouds like oranges and drink down the juice They rub their faces with icebergs They lie naked on frozen snow My thirst multiplies remultiplies I would give rubies for a drop of ice-water My tongue is a fire-brand My body is the heat of a hundred hells My eyes are red coins of burning coal My hair is a forest fire There is the roar of a conflagration Is it the echo of the sun? Is it the thunder of the waves of the sun pounding against the ramparts of my heart? Am I this ribbon of fire hanging like a pigtail from the Sun crackling in a hot wind of madness?

[*The Morada* 2, Winter 1930]

ASSASSIN

(voici le temps des assassins —Rimbaud)
(unleash the sword and fire —Shelley)

I exchange eyes with the Mad Queen

the mirror crashes against my face and
bursts into a thousand suns
all over the city flags crackle and bang
fog horns scream in the harbor
the wind hurricanes through the window
and I begin to dance the dance of the
Kurd shepherds

    I stamp upon the floor
    I whirl like dervishes
colors revolve dressing and undressing
I lash them with fury
stark white with iron black
harsh red with blue
marble green with bright orange
and only gold remains naked
columns of steel rise and plunge
emerge and disappear
pistoning in the river of my soul
    thrusting upwards
    thrusting downwards
    thrusting inwards
    thrusting outwards
        penetrating

I roar with joy
black-footed ferrets disappear into holes

the sun tattooed on my back
begins to spin
        faster and faster
        whirring whirring
throwing out a glory of sparks
sparks shoot off into space
sparks into shooting stars
shooting stars collide with comets

        Explosions
      Naked Colors Explode
           into
       Red Disaster

I crash out through the
window naked, widespread
upon a
      Heliosaurus
I uproot an obelisk and plunge
it into the ink-pot of the
Black Sea
I write the word

    SUN

across the dreary palimpsest
of the world
I pour contents of the

Red Sea down my throat
I erect catapults and
lay siege to the cities of the world
I scatter violent disorder
throughout the kingdoms of the world
I stone the people of the world
I stride over mountains
I pick up oceans like thin cards
and spin them into oblivion
I kick down walled cities
I hurl giant firebrands against governments
I thrust torches through the eyes of the law
        I annihilate museums
        I demolish libraries
        I oblivionize skyscrapers
I become hard as adamant
strong as battle
indurated in solid fire
rigid with hatred

I bring back the wizards and the sorcerers
the necromancers
the magicians
I practise witchcraft
I set up idols
with a sharp edged sword
I cut through the crowded streets
comets follow in my wake
stars make obeisance to me
the moon uncovers her
nakedness to me

I am the harbinger of a
New Sun World
I bring the Seed of a
    New Copulation
I proclaim the Mad Queen

I stamp out vast empires
I crush palaces in my rigid
    hands
I harden my heart against
    churches

I blot out cemeteries
I feed the people with
stinging nettles
I resurrect madness
I thrust my naked sword
between the ribs of the world
I murder the world !

[*Pagany*, Vol. I, No. I, Winter 1930]

THE ROSE

to fame unknown
to many a, and many a maid
we are not naming
to whom was given
virtue
(be as wax to flaming)
we poets in our desire
wear the rose of what he steals from her
learning in the freshness of
ashes cold as fire

OUR FEET

our feet are nailed to desperate paths
our feet are bruised
our feet endure
contending with
crossed with
a man I am
what way to endure
our feet because of yours are pure

SLEEPING TOGETHER

cry in your sleep and implore
cry autumn's fire still small
cry as the door to the wind
cry for I call
cry for the touch of the snow upon snow
cry of the things that you fear
cry in the darkness a distant
    dream in my ear

SHARING FIRE

white as a thought of
whiteness
pure in thought as are
sad as said to be the speech of
those who sharing fire
teach us it is growing late
teach us to inquire
at the heavy gate

ROOTS

tall ancestral
tongues in
unto the root of
dark-fingered
as the needle to the pole
as the shadow to the sun
fungi and mushrooms
and the root of a tree
dark-fingered
thrusting into
infinity

CŒUR DE JEUNE FEMME

her heart
is of a number of things
of whispered song
of comfort built with money
of dead men's bones
of necklaces and rings
of faith
(he was fresh and funny
of good intentions
of good works
of goodly prospect
of grace force
     fascination youth)
her heart is of marble
her defence
of sweet indifferencce
when he proposes

VENUS

made up of loveliness
looking in the looking-glass
ample room and verge enough
flesh in the glass

never anything can be
frail as her coquetry
analytic with a glance
Venus rouges for the dance

anchors great and anchors small
hold her lovers fast in thrall
apparitions seen with scorn
one is gone

MIRACLE

abysm of time, dark
abysmal dark, or the
abyss, into this wild
accent of an angel's whisper
accents flow with artless ease
that are ours,
accept a miracle instead of these

RECKON THE DAYS

reckon the days you have not been
anticipate the past
ye evening tapers
reckon the days
iron shall cool at last
reckon the days in one word
reckon the past

INVOCATION TO THE SUN-GODDESS

I would you were the hollow ship
fashioned to bear the cargo of my love
the unrelenting glove
hurled in defiance at our blackest world
or that great banner mad unfurled
the poets plant upon the hill of time
or else amphora for the gold of life
liquid and naked as a virgin wife

       Yourself the Prize
       I gird with Fire
       The Great White Ruin
       Of my Desire.
       I burn to gold
fierce and unerring as a conquering sword
       I burn to gold
fierce and undaunted as a lion lord
       seeking your bed
and leave to them the
       burning of the dead

[*Unrest : The Rebel Poets' Anthology for 1929*]

SCORN

you business men with your large desks, with your stenographers and your bell-boys and your private telephones, I say to you these are the four walls of your cage.

you are tame as canaries with your small bird-brains where lurks the evil worm, you are fat from being over-fed, you know not the lean wild sunbirds that arrow down paths of fire.

I despise you, I am too hard to pity you, I would hang you on the gallows of the Stock Exchange, I would flay you with taxes, I would burn you alive with Wall Street Journals, I would condemn you to an endless round of bank banquets, I deride you, I mock at you, I laugh you to scorn.

[*Unrest : The Rebel Poets' Anthology for 1930*]

photo of Caresse Crosby and her whippet, Clitoris

SLEEPING TOGETHER
A BOOK OF DREAMS (*These dreams for Caresse*)

" fermons les yeux pour voir "

" Again, if two lie together, then they have heat, but how can one be warm alone ? "
 ECCLESIASTES

INSPECTION

A ferocious animal breaks suddenly into our new bathroom where we are disporting ourselves in a hot bath. I can recall your expression of contempt at the intrusion but although you threw the nailbrush and the cake of soap at him and although I made use of a golf club (I believe it was a silver cleek) we were not able to beat him into submission and we were compelled to submit to a sly and searching inspection which evinced on the part of the ferocious animal more than one exclamation of surprise.

GIRLS UNDER TEN

I begin to take it as a matter of course that no girl under ten years can in any circumstances swim more than a given number of strokes and naturally when the whole question has become one of formula I am not surprised when the girls look up at me and drown without more than a perfunctory show of resistance but you can imagine my horror when the last of the little girls looks up at me through eyes that could never be any but your own.

ON THE GROUNDS OF INDECENCY

A giraffe is gorging himself on your lace garters a Parisian doll is washing herself in my tall glass of gin fizz while I insist on their eletrocution on the grounds of indecency.

WE HAVE FORGOTTEN OUR CALLING-CARDS

The man in the moon is as rose-colored as our finger-nails as we go hand in hand into the garden you and I to somewhere beyond the sleeping roses but although you remove your silk stockings and I my silk socks (we have forgotten our calling-cards) the star butler with his silver tray never reappears and we are forced to find our way home along the bottom of the lake.

NO INDICATION OF WHERE I MIGHT FIND YOU

I am kissing a name on a wall when a little takeyourhandaway girl appears from behind the aerodrome. She tells me you told her to tell me to tell her to tell you the name of the taxicab driver who was accused of kissing a horse (giving no reason for this strange request) the absurdity of this dream being no more than averagely characteristic of the sleeping state although it was far from a pleasant dream in that the little girl disappeared behind the aerodrome without giving me any indication of where I might find you.

GAME OF TAG

I am astonished at the remarkable erudition of the art critic who is seated upon a high mountain of catalogues from which he is haranguing a regiment of bespectacled students on the superiority of contemporary French painters over the masters of the past. He is bold and daring in his assertions. He is eloquence at its zenith. But I prefer to go on with a game of tag which I am playing with you on the hot sands of a beach feeling the electric touch of your fingers on my naked shoulders, hearing the hilarity of mockery in your laughter, pursuing the mad impulsiveness of your body as you dodge back and forth like white strokes from the brush of an artist.

PERFORMANCE BY TWO

Your woman's name is a sharp diamond scratching little animals on the red mirror of my heart whose greed for the fruit of a certain tree is accentuated by the essential qualities of our lust. O impetuous performance by two ! ... And now, although you step proudly, although you carry a staff of authority in your hand, although you are followed by more than one attendant, I need no garment for protection, no quantity of swords to split the way, no chariot of fire, for I have already plundered the floating petals from the flower-mill of your body, this victory having been brought about by the putting up of a very hard doctrine in the game of war.

I AM IN YOUR SOUL

I am in your soul (as all lovers live and sleep in a certain sense in their beloved's soul) among the frail crumpled garments of your thought cast here and there in disarray by invisible hands (are they yours are they mine or are they perhaps the eager hands of time) the fallen petals of your apparel symbolic of your former vagaries, the dress discarded on the floor of your imagination the discarded robe of your past, your red slippers petulantly kicked into a corner of your brain like a pair of red-throated scruples, the broken girdle at your waist for a sign of desire, slender ribbons to suggest slender nights of love slenderer than crescent moons at dawn, while all your hair becomes a mysterious undercurrent flowing through me the new current of fire pulsating through my arteries, but the pleasantest part of this dream is my awakening at the white hour before sunrise to find you sleeping by my side.

UNREMOVED BY RUBBING

A black and yellow bird morbidly tender with a feminine name excites, by her musical exercises, one of a Jewish sect who lies on a portable bed among a thicket of white wind-flowers but, in spite of his entreaties, she is unyielding, and he is forced to resume his relations (lascivious) with a corpulent Spanish Lady the back of whose neck I have marked with my teeth (there is no need to be jealous) much to the consternation of a young Miss Eraser who, until now, had labored under the delusion that everything could be removed by rubbing.

MOSQUITO

Let us go to our friend the mosquito and ask him if he will transfer one little crimson corpuscle from you to me one little crimson corpuscle from me to you in order to effect a mystic communication which will make our two hearts one. In exchange for his services we can offer to shelter him from the wind, in exchange for his services we can offer to steep him in liquid honey, in exchange for his services we can rescue him from the snare of the spiderweb. So that I was not astonished when I woke up to find that we were covered with mosquito bites for we had forgotten the white netting (we were in Venice) but in spite of having the mosquito at my mercy (he was too drowsy-drunk to fly away) I preferred to let him live and instead wreaked my vengeance on a swarm of wasps that infested our breakfast table.

OVID'S FLEA

The arching of your neck, the curve of your thigh, the hollow under your arm, the posture of your body, are more than anodynes throughout the length of my dream but although I have the power to be bright and wild I am baffled in my desire for absolute possession and I am forced to compare myself to Ovid's flea who could creep into every corner of a wench but could in no wise endanger her virginity.

CAT

I am a lean Siamese cat who insists upon sleeping under our bed in order to watch the mouse-holes so I am not as astonished as you are when I wake up next morning to find myself under our bed.

GAZELLE AT LUNCHEON

So saying (but of what you said I was never very certain) you came dashing across the room as you spoke and flung the door open revealing to me a somewhat odd scene. A gazelle dressed as a girl (I seemed to recognize several articles of your apparel) was rapidly eating all the ten dollar bills (profits from New Moon's great victory at Longchamp, alas, only a dream victory) which we had hidden so cleverly (or so we had thought) in your green-and-white douche bag which the maid had evidently forgotten to put away, but in spite of our entreaties we were unable to persuade the gazelle (she answered to the name Ionduile) to abandon the rest of her meal and we were obliged to watch in despair (we were riveted in one place as one so often is in dreams without the power to move) until the last orange-colored bill had disappeared down her throat.

THEY THE TWELVE LIONS

They the twelve lions prowl swiftly on a long silver tunnel and the entire dream is a waiting to be devoured but contrary to all the laws of reason this waiting to be devoured is not a terrifying nightmare sensation but on the contrary a delightful one the only out about it being the discussion we are having as to who is to have the privilege of being devoured by Rahla the Lioness. The subject of the dream which seemed to occupy an eternity although I suppose it took place in a few seconds is not difficult to explain for it is hardly a week ago that we went together to see our friend the lion-tamer at the little circus under the tent.

ONE HUNDRED WAYS OF KISSING GIRLS

A rabbit-dealer is looking into a rabbit's mouth and examining its teeth but you are far more interested in the young cripple who holds up a wax leg for me to light as I would light a candle and by the light of his flaming leg I can read the book of one hundred ways of kissing girls which he has been able to buy with the selling of his large stock of artificial eyes stolen from the top drawer of your grandmother's dressing-table but unfortunately when I woke up I couldn't remember even half the number of ways of kissing girls and alas the little book had vanished with the dream.

SUNRISE EXPRESS

I am endeavoring to persuade a Chinese professor who is at work on a torpedo which he expects to shoot to the sun to allow us to live in the centre of this torpedo but he insists that there is no room for our double bed and that we shall have to sleep as sailors do in a hammock which is discouraging in view of the length of the journey.

I HAD NO IDEA WHAT THEY WOULD DO NEXT

I think it began by my pouring the coffee into the sugar bowl while you sitting up in bed with a mirror in your hand were humming your impossible melodies. I knew too that as soon as the sugar melted the white rain would begin to beat against the window. Outside a tree was dying at its roots but I was much more fascinated by the whiteness of your hands for I had no idea what they would do next. There seemed to be an inner light with sugar-squares of shadow outside and I seemed to be awaiting a reply in your eyes which I did not receive until I woke up and found them looking into mine.

HE CALLED US A GIRL

To be by ourselves to grow together to become entangled so that the gayly dressed tax-collector who used to take charge of the black beetles at the insect-zoo would tax us as being one. He called us a girl which I did not resent for we only had to contribute one pineapple instead of two crocodiles. He uttered an insect cry and departed in his phaeton drawn by nine thousand nine hundred and ninety-nine black beetles one black beetle having escaped into the jar of raspberry jam which we had inadvertently left on the piazza.

MIRACULOUS MESSAGE

I am in a parlor car. I am in a dining car. I am in a sleeping car. I have the upper berth so that I cannot look out the window but I have the apprehensive feeling of things happening in the dark outside. A bearded creature carrying a telegram in his mouth as a dog often carries a newspaper is trying to get on the train. I know in advance it is for me believing what I cannot prove. I feel that I am indivisible with the telegram but I am not able to put my hand through the steel side of the car. I have already decided to hide it under the roof of my tongue when I am sleepily aware of a body stirring in my arms and of the utter uselessness of the telegram which could not possibly contain such a miraculous message as your " Are you awake Dear."

WHITE AEROPLANES IN FLIGHT

We are flying. Below us the land is a sheet of notepaper scrawled over by the words of roads and rivers. A cemetery is a game of chess. A ploughed field is an accordeon. Black hayricks are crows. We are one of an astonishing pack of white aeroplanes a million million in number filling the sky with a myriad white points of light hunting after the red fox of the sun. We lose him among the clouds. We find him again. But he eludes us and burrows out of sight into the blue tunnel of the sea and you and I are confronted by the unpleasant problem of having to alight in the Place Vendome because we must cash a cheque at the bank before we can take a room at the Ritz. We awake to a bang. It is the femme de chambre closing the windows of our room while Narcisse is barking to be let out.

ANIMAL MAGNETISM

All the sailors are laughing. It is contagious. All the whores are yawning. It is contagious. And all night long we wear ourselves out trying to laugh and yawn at one and the same time.

SAINT VALENTINE'S NIGHT

It is Saint Valentine's Night and you are jumping up and down like a jack-in-the-box with the bright toy of my heart in your hand.

YOUR EYES ARE THE REAL EYES

I see the gold coins of me scattered along the road to the sun. I see myself a decade ago a year ago a month ago a day ago in various fixed scenes like a photograph in an album like a portrait in a gallery but the nicest part about this dream is that in every photograph in every portrait your face looks out from the upper right-hand corner of the picture as if you were the artist who had painted the portrait with the desire to appear in it yourself. The strange thing is that your eyes are your real eyes as in those old paintings made with holes for the eyes behind which people could conceal themselves and look out unseen on what was happening around them.

NAKED LADY IN A YELLOW HAT

You are the naked lady in the yellow hat.

CUE OF WIND

Red funnels are vomiting tall smoke plumes gold and onyx and diamond and emerald into four high round circles which solidify before they collide together with the impact of billiard balls that soon are caromed by a thin cue of wind into the deep pockets of our sleep.

C C

P.S. the maid never returned to turn down the bed each word illuminated in a different color but all the other pages of your letter (my fingers inform me that there are a great many of them) are as blank as the ceiling of our bedroom white as the linen sheets except for the strange last page P.S. the maid never returned to turn down the bed nor can I find out why you wrote this letter (nor why you signed yourself Cunningest Concubine) not can I ever know what bed you refer to (we have slept in so many beds) nor who the maid is who never chooses to return.

IT IS SNOWING

We are preparing ourselves for the horrors of war by viewing an autopsy. A trained nurse depressingly capable sits by a stove reading aloud from the Madonna of the Sleeping Cars while you insist on telling me that for three years the chorus girls have not come to Touggourt. There is a turmoil of passionate red except for my hands which are two drifts of white snow lying upon the cool shells of your breasts. It is snowing and there are people in galoshes and when we wake up it is snowing and there is the sound of the men shovelling the snow off the sidewalks. It is one of those cold grey days when the wise thing for us to do is to go to sleep again like bears in the wintertime.

VERY NICE TO LOOK AT AND SWEET TO TOUCH

I have said goodbye to you and have gone shopping. I am thinking very seriously of buying a new searchlight for the lighthouse of my brain when I see a large sign in a shop window across the street Very Nice To Look At And Sweet To Touch under which I see sitting up in a little red-and-silver bed alert and done up in ribbons like a Christmas present your own sweet self but my joy is short-lived for I immediately realize that even if I sell my entire supply of snowballs polo balls tennis balls and gold balls I should not have enough even to buy one of your eyebrows. At this moment an ugly old man steps out of his Rolls-Royce and enters the shop. I follow him knife in hand a riot in my heart but my extreme anguish must have awakened me for the next thing I remember is Narcisse who has encroached on the bed licking my hand in token of good morning.

YOU ARE STANDING ON YOUR HEAD

You are standing on top of your head on the ping-pong table in front of the house while I encourage your performance. My eyes plunder the red roses of your toes. My gestures are marked by emotion. My hands are alive in expectation of your fall. My enthusiasm is unbounded. But what right has the sun to make hot declaration to you. What right has the gardener with dandruff to blunder through the gate. What right has the wind to unbalance you so that you sway like a lily-plant. And still you balance yourself upon your head observing at all times the most perfect equanimity. And still you kindle in me the excitement of danger. But whether you fell or not I shall never know for the negro conductor at that moment stuck his head into our compartment and shouted New York.

STREET OF THE FOUR WINDS

We are together in the Street of the Four Winds wondering what will happen next. In a shopwindow a baby baboon is being born. I insist that you buy the white summer dress that hangs in the flowershop. A miniature clipper ship mounted on roller skates rattles past us over the cobblestones. A man with a pair of pyjamas under his derby hat (I can see the white streamers floating in the wind) walks into the Hotel Cometobed with a woman dressed in a fur coat who looks as if she ought to be milked. We buy the white summer dress. You put it on over your blue dress for the races and we walk rapidly down the street and into a church where we listen to a choir of U. S. Debutantes singing The Empty Bed Blues. It is difficult to imagine the degree of sharpness obtained in this dream.

QUEEN OF HEARTS

I do not find it strange that a bluebird should fall in love with the playing card you hold in your hand because the playing card in question happens to be the queen of hearts.

WHITE ERMINE

I am being warned of a danger but the female kangaroo who is looking earnestly into space will not tell me nor will the passengers on the omnibus who are counting their small cubes of silver tell me nor will the dunce standing in the corner of the Ritz Bar tell me nor will Mr. Tunney not will the Italian girl with the Irish name nor will the notary public nor will my friend the chief of forty thieves tell me nor even the puffed-up interpreter who squanders understanding between two countries, so I am entirely unprepared to meet the danger which I seek to evade by the stubborn adherence to an object of phallic reverence which I am able to extract from the glands of the wingèd insect which you always wear as a clasp for your coat of white ermine.

MIRACLE OF THE TOOTH

By some miracle possibly only in a dream I have become one of your teeth. It is with me that you bite into the lusciousness of a peach. It is with me you crunch the piece of toast covered with caviar. It is with me you nibble at your ear of corn on the cob. But my pleasure is not as great as you may suppose for the dentist in need of money has told you that I must be pulled out and I am tortured by the uncertainty of your decision.

C PREFERRED

I am standing before the giant blackboard of the Stock Exchange torn between desires. It is an era of wild speculation. Your Breasts picked up casually three years ago at 88 are now selling three hundred glittering points above that mark. Nombril Bonds have gone up. Shares in your Eyes of Blue have almost risen out of reach. The market is cornered as regards your Legs. Your Mouth Preferred has soared to new heights and I am placed in the predicament of having to sell everything in order to buy your Heart.

A PROGRESS UPWARD

Occurring at rare intervals is a dream of fairy-tale lightness more swift than the flight of tennis balls. This dream consists of a progress upward towards a light metallic fire (sweet-smelling as a sun-ray) which pours like honey into a minute orifice rigidly exact whose organ of hearing is adjusted to the harmony of your hands.

THE RED UMBRELLA

It is the beginning and the end of the world one infinitesimal grain of sand swells and swells and swells and swells until it is an enormous circular beach which suddenly tilts and slides down into the sea leaving us clinging to the handle of your red umbrella which is automatically opening and shutting against a windy sky (I notice the stars have all been blown away) but nothing more happens for I feel in my ears the insistent burring of the alarm clock and the even more insistent challenge of your mouth.

I WAS NEVER HAPPIER

The activity of my hands unbuttoning your jacket remind me of the white accuracy of a machine. You are murmuring something to me about a feast of dolls. A little doll comes out of a doll-house. You make such a happy face it said and she sleeps on your arm. I feel very shy as we kiss at the foot of the rainbow but you reassure me with the white-caps of your smile which break against the shoreline of my mouth. I was never happier although I have the feeling of not being able to wait very long between drinks. You keep whispering to me that Roma written backwards spells Amor.

SAFETY-PIN

Audaciously you put on the hat belonging to the lady and walk with me down the abrupt declivity to the sea. A large body of water confronts us whereon is no ship wherein is no fish (so we are told by the skeleton of the fisherman) so that we are spared the anxiety of sharks. You are preparing to undress and are taking off your rings preparatory to putting them in the conch-shell which I hold up to you. You are having difficulties with a safety-pin while I remain an appreciative spectator. We are interrupted by the four winds whistling together over the burial of the dead but though we searched up and down the beach we found no corpse and we were forced or rather you were forced to return to the problem of the safety-pin which refused to open for the simple reason that your fingers were inadequate to the occasion.

SOLUTION OF A MYSTERY

I am breaking white stones (it is curious how the color white plays such an important part in my dreams) in an island off China (I know it is China for they are throwing a corpse to the dogs) because I seriously wish to build a road which will follow the solution of a mystery that concerns itself with the young needle-woman who is zealously sewing garments for us to wear at the six-day bicycle race on the day of the New Moon.

REVIRGINATE

A swift metallic monster with eyes more precious than diamonds rich in the secrets of sun and wind whirs with the whizzing sound of an arrow into the direct center of my dream from which you turn sleepily with what *is* the matter what *is* the matter until we both fall asleep again under your grey squirrel coat which I pull over our heads for it is bitter cold.

HUMAN FLESH AND GOLDEN APPLES

Like the horses of Diomedes I am being nourished with human flesh while you are eating the golden apples of the Hesperides. I suppose they are the apples of the Hesperides for they are so very big and gold. There is a clean sound of gravel being raked. The shadows under your eyes are blue as incense. Your voice is the distant crying of night-birds, your body is the long white neck of the peacock as she comes down the gravel path. Your mouth is an acre of desire so much as may be kissed in a day, our love the putting together of parts of an equation, so that when they knocked on the door at nine o'clock I could not believe that you were in the country and I alone in a hotel in New York forced to take consolation in the bottle of white rum that I bought last night from the elevator boy.

AERONAUTICS

There is a tree too high for me to reach its top until the young girl (I can tell it is you you are wearing furs and a veil) proposes that we take flying lessons whereupon I climb to the top of the tree and set at liberty my soul but when I slide down again to the ground you are disappearing out of sight on a tricycle and I am powerless to climb back again, the funny part about this dream being that yesterday I took my first flying lesson.

GIRLS ARE CLIMBING

Girls are climbing up and down ladders. Boys stand below holding the ladders steady. One ladder leads to a hayloft. It is not ours. Another leads to the top of a tower. It is not ours. A third leads to a house in a tree. It is not ours. A fourth leads to the top of a flagpole. It is not ours, for ours is a rope ladder whose every knot is a star and whose end is securely fastened to the horn of the little crescent moon whose astonishment at our sudden appearance is reduced from an excessive degree to a minor one when we present her with a bottle of Coty's gardenia with which she perfumes herself to the great satisfaction of her lesbian friend the dawn girl who soon appears dressed in an expensive peignoir of pink clouds.

YOU WERE TRYING TO TELL ME SOMETHING

I carry hay on a horse which I shall use to prepare our bed which is marked like the ace in a pack of cards with the number one. You sit crooked upon your legs as tailors do at the foot of the bed gazing intently at the wallpaper whereon the sign of the arrow is marked in white. A sunshade lies across a book of hymns which I do not dare open for fear of disturbing the wild geese whose cry extends like an elastic band from ocean to ocean. I remember being very nervous for fear the elastic band would break. You were trying to tell me something but of what you said I was never very sure although I think it was something to do with fishes closing their eyes when they sleep. When I awoke it was with a feeling of loneliness which was intensified by the fact that you had already gone to take your cold bath.

THE CRAMOISY QUEEN

We are leaning up against our bar at the Mill. I am drinking down as many glasses of gin as there are letters in your name. The taste of gin is in my mouth and on my tongue a great and amorous speech. I feel trumpets within me. I put on my coat of gold and lead you by the hand. The Cramoisy Queen The Cramoisy Queen Taratantara Taratantara but you are crying and I realize for the hundredth time that women will always in the long run be reducible to tears.

DICE IN A YELLOW SKULL

I am rattling dice in a yellow skull they are falling upon the snow at the feet of the plump woman with bare breasts who is absorbed in the passion of giving milk to a rattlesnake but when the numbers on the face of the dice correspond to the numbers of birds of paradise that form the jewels of her necklace she withdraws behind a white counterpane for the purpose of concealment and we are left alone to finish our game of strip poker.

WHITE CLOVER

There is a clairvoyance of white clover, a coming towards me of the white star-fish of your feet, an aeolus of drapery. Your hand on the knob of the door is the timidity of the new moon, your hair over your shoulders a cataract of unloosened stars, your slender arms the white sails you lift to the mast of my neck. Not even the silkiness of new-drawn milk can compare to your skin, not even the cool curves of amphora can compare to the cool curves of your breasts, not even the epithalamiumic gestures of an Iseult can compare to your queenliness. Your ears are the littlest birds for the arrows of my voice, your lap the innocent resting place for the hands of my desire. And as you sit nude and shy on the edge of our bed I wonder at the miracle of the opening of your eyes.

CRUEL MOUTH AND LITTLE EAR

Stuffed birds are stuffed souls snakes in bottles are dead phalluses but I cannot see why this should be a reason for me to feed red peanuts to a menagerie of stars while the cruel mouth of the sun (in this case my own) whispers intimacies into the little crescent ear of the moon (which is undoubtedly your little ear).

I FOLLOW YOU TO BED

You bite repeatedly one of the white leaves of a flower no doubt because you are jealous of my playing at marbles with a slender long-legged girl who turns out to be the granddaughter of Helen of Troy. Somewhere to our left a female servant is converting a pleasure-boat into a floating bed. She takes down the white-colored sails she makes them smooth and even, in order to use them as sheets. She makes a mattress by tying together the softest fishing-nets. She snares two living life-preservers winds them round with silk ribbons and uses them for pillows. I am indifferent to the game of marbles for I prefer to watch you eat your white leaf. The granddaughter of Helen of Troy is saying something about the largest gland of the human body while you argue (between mouthfuls) in favor of the great artery of the heart. I make a choice and having abandoned the game of marbles I follow you to bed but imagine my surprise when I woke up to find we were not in bed as I had supposed but lying half-dressed under the shelter of a sand dune while the late afternoon sun rolled like a great golden marble down the sky.

FOR THE PREVENTION OF CRUELTY TO BRIDES

Inasmuch as your eyes your hands your feet your breasts are natural objects of worship I refuse to accept the marks for bad behavior which the semi-exhausted professor who is lecturing on love to the Young Women's Society For The Prevention Of Cruelty To Brides insists on giving me. I bristle with rage like a battleship with guns. I call forth invectives. Old Flowerpot I think I called him. My tongue is sharper than a cutting tool but as sharp as the young woman's laughter. I am not a newcomer. I am not an undergraduate. I am not as layman, not a dilettante, not a monk. Let him go on with his lecture with which he barely earns his living while I who regard pleasure as the chief good shall return quickly to your eyes your hands your feet your breasts experiencing in my dream all the singular phenomena which result from the confused sensations of touch during sleep.

I BREAK WITH THE PAST

In a hot office building a man is dictating a letter to a bright-eyed stenographer who has just graduated from the College of Progress. Dear Madam I regret to inform you that your swans have sleeping-sickness, but I am far away in the country wandering across the golf links your bright-colored scarf around my neck. I cannot seem to find you. I look into every bunker. I ask the caddy with the gluttonous face. I call out loud to the birds. I keep remembering how good-looking you are with your bedroom eyes and your new-moon ears. I begin to run. It is growing late for the red wolf of the sun has almost disappeared into his cavern of night. I run over the wooden bridge. I break with the past and race into the future over the far end of the links feeling myself fly through the air towards two sensations of light which turn out to be your eyes. When I wake up I am as tired as a marathon runner.

GOLDEN SPOON

Your body is the golden spoon by means of which I eat your soul. I do not seek to find the explanation for this curious sensation which is more visual than tactile. But I am afraid of the army of silver spoons marshaled in array under their commander-in-chief Silver Fork who is about to give the command to march against the golden spoon which I hold desperately in my mouth.

SEESAW

We are playing at seesaw you and I and it is much more exhilarating than the usual game for our plank is so long (I can just make you out in the distance a patch of cramoisy against the white of clouds) that we are able to rise as high as the top of the sky. The game consists of how many stars we can unhook we each carry a basket on our left arm for that purpose when the telephone rang. As we woke up I remembered that I was leading, having caught seventy-seven to your seventy-three, but you were protesting on the score that your stars were the brightest stars.

FOR A PROTECTION

I see part of your face part of your mouth moving in salutation making amends for the light wind that unravels your hair. I realize that the snowball I am bringing to you for a plaything is inadequate. There is for background a white colonnade a mere incident in the measure of the dream which is brought to a close by your turning into a heavy silk fabric which I wind around me as a protection against the cold wind which no doubt made itself felt in my dream because all our bedclothes had fallen off during the night.

WHITE FIRE

Your throat in my dream is a sensation of light so bright so sudden that I am dominated by the image of white fire far beyond the moment of ordinary awakening.

AUNT AGATHA

A leg should be more than a leg you said and I agreed. There are caterpillars underfoot you said and I agreed for I could feel my bare feet squashing a liquid something. The secret of love is to be animalistic you said and I agreed for I like panthers. But when you said let us go to call on Aunt Agatha I toed you face downward across a chair, turned up your clothes with the utmost precision and was just on the point of lashing you with a silver switch when there was a shriek of laughter as the Gay Duchess and Elsa de Brabent burst into the room to tell us that their niece Little Lady Lightfoot had been expelled from school for having been caught in the act of kissing the Yellow Dwarf. Here the dream ended for I felt you pressing knowingly into my arms and I realized that it must be long after seven to judge by the position of the sun as reflected in the twin mirrors of your eyes.

RITZ TOWER

The Ritz Tower sways like a drunkard under the cold fire of the moon while you sit in your lace pyjamas at the edge of the bed busily cutting your toe-nails to the great astonishment of a bottle of gin which stares out at you from behind a pair of my white tennis shoes.

WHITE STOCKINGS

Your white stockings spread to dry on the station platform of some rural station whose clock announces that it is noon are the cause of the station-master's suicide whose bones the locomotive crunches as a dog crunches a chicken-bone. I remember being surprised that the hands of the clock which were almost as slender as your own never moved and that in spite of a hot sun your stockings were still damp when you went to put them on after the tea-party.

WHITE SLIPPER

A white aeroplane whiter than the word Yes falls like a slipper from the sky. You come dancing over the silver thorns of the lawn and by holding up the corners of your rose-and-white skirt you catch the white slipper which I kick down to you from the sun.

ONE LETTER OF THE ALPHABET

The crescent moon—such a short dream such a frail fragment of broken memory such a silver against silver frail fantasy burnt lightly bright and delicate into the whiteness of my brain.

IN PURSUIT OF YOUR EYES

All night I dream I am an eagle winging over deserts of insanity in pursuit of the drunken birds of your eyes but although this has been a recurring dream I have never succeeded in catching both birds in the same night on night it is the left eye on another the right but last night for the first time (let this be a good omen) the eagle overtook and devoured both of the birds at once and this morning I have the sensation of a complete virginity of victory.

[*American Caravan* IV, 1931]

Horse Race

Heliopolis Park Chart

(By the Associated Press)

Thursday January Seventeenth Seventh Day
    Weather Clear Track Fast
Fourth Race The Sunfire Stakes
One Hundred Thousand Dollars and a Gold Cup
    All Ages A Mile and a Furlong

    1 Mad Queen
    2 Infuriate
    3 Firecracker
    4 Rackarock

Also Ran : Agitator Inebriate Detonator Loop the Loop Red Flag Cannoncracker The Lunatic Incendiary Hurricane Feu d'Artifice Thundercrash Folastre Wild Party Turmoil Typhoon The Suicide Whirlwind Storm Cloud The Anarchist Nymphomaniac.

Scratched : Safety First Sobriety Keep off the Grass. Dolly Doldrums Equanimity Law Enforcement. Senility The Sentimentalist Wet Blanket. The Eunuch Watch Your Step Weak Sister.

Start Good Won Driving Place Same. Winner by Sunstroke out of Storm Queen. Jockey H. H. Maniak Trainer Eugene Winner Owner Lord Sun. Time 0.21.4, 0.22.2, 0.24.

Up to Win in Last Stride

Mad Queen on the outside worked up fast and closing gamely was up to win in the last stride. Infuriate was pinched back on the turn but came again and finished fast. Firecracker was in close quarters all the way. Rackarock ran a good race. Nymphomaniac was last.

[*An Anthology of the Younger Poets*, 1932]

Invocation to the Mad Queen

I would you were the hollow ship
fashioned to bear the cargo of my love
the unrelenting glove
hurled in defiance at our blackest world
or that great banner mad unfurled
the poet plants upon the hill of time
or else amphora for the gold of life
liquid and naked as a virgin wife.

    Yourself the Prize
    I gird with Fire
    The Great White Ruin
    Of my Desire.

    I burn to gold
fierce and unerring as a conquering sword
    I burn to gold
fierce and undaunted as a lion lord
    seeking your Bed
and leave to them the
    burning of the dead.

[*An Anthology of the Younger Poets,* 1932]

In Madness

not in calm weather
faint breezes calm summer
when clouds have fled from the sky
and she lies with her hair and her dress undone
asleep in the hay in the sun
frail as a feather
I say not in this weather

but when the trees are bare
when the wind roars
when it whirls up the grass
      on the ground
when it drives the rain forward
when the sound of the thunder
      and slamming of doors
warns of mad weather
I say in this weather
(black out of doors
black meadows
black raindrops
black weather)
in this weather
when the storm is howling across the sky
then shall the Mad Queen fly to her love
proud as a feather
proud as sun
their hearts mad beating
      in unison

[*An Anthology of the Younger Poets*, 1932]

Empty Bed Blues

Once she reached upward for the Stars took them quite bravely in her hands and scattered them upon the bed of love — a double bed a flowerbed a bridal bed (for moments when her love burned red) a bed of gold where frantic wild and uncontrolled she moved her limbs and wed, a mad a frantic all-tempestuous bed, a bed where flames of love were swiftly fed neither with butter eggs nor bread but with eyes and arms and breasts and knees with thighs and legs that moved and squeezed with hands and feet and things half said with trees and roses stiff and red, a bed that led to naked sleep a bed that held mad queens asleep with arms encircling strong to keep a oneness even in their sleep, a bed where hearts beat red as dawn, a bed that saw their poor forlorn and tired bodies greet the dawn, a bed that knew the dread of that black hour just ahead when tired lovers pale and dead rose wearily and as they fled glanced backwards at their empty bed.

[*An Anthology of the Younger Poets*, 1932]

Water-Lilies

Unwedded from the world, I stray through trees
To where a pool lies mirrored in the Sun
A disk of polished gold that I have won
With labours not unknown to Hercules.

Slender they bathe, all naked as a breeze,
Their nipples hollow and their hair undone,
While from their widespread thighs cool ripples run
To rock the water-lilies round their knees.

Nymphs of the fountains, naiads innocent,
Frail sunbeams who have passed between my arms
So beautiful in your imprisonment,
Fill now my soul with symbols of delight :
Soft voices and soft fingers and soft charms
And the curving of a darkness into light.

[*An Anthology of the Younger Poets*, 1932]

Quatrains to the Sun

I

A sunfort flourished in my sunless heart
Beyond the Sun. Here in a tower apart
The sunbirds of my lady's eyes were caged
Alas, poor targets for the sun-god's dart.

II

The Sun at Chartres seen through an open door
Was like a nest, wherein I hatched a score
Of red-gold sun-thoughts. Now unheralded
They change to sun-nymphs on my heart's dark shore.

III

The sun at noon is like a pool of gold
Towards whose uncertain brink the clouds have rolled
To quench their thirst. Likewise invisible winds
Drink fire, and all my heart is sun-consoled.

IV

Like to a giant dragon in his cage
Of clouds the Sun in unconcealed rage
Glares down across the magic of the world
Intent upon this untried pasturage.

V

The Sun is a red arrow plunged to rest
In the dark target of the sea's wild breast
But morning shall unveil the gentle scene
Of sun-girls bathing in a palimpsest.

[*An Anthology of the Younger Poets*, 1932]

Sunstroke

each Color changed her dress
and notions difficult to dream
(when pencils play there
parts preponderous)
tanged Sunward
with ladies proffering
their breasts

no yeast suggests the
ruffled tenor of the
dragoman
who wishes on the hay
one last encounter
irrelevant of pause
(why change her drawers
to make the rhyme
less difficult to see)

the soot on ivory carpets
mongol-colored in the brain
the bitter rain
beyond the destination
of the heart
beyond the destination
of the brain

beyond the destination
of the brain
the sleeping goat-bugs
know not any avatar
and where the Russian

orifice is samovar
there Red Sea Rimbaud
guards his Aden Caravan
and Verlaine trembles
to the touch of trains

      it rains
      it rains
to mourn the ocean giants
buried deep
among the rankled seaweed
sharp with frost (aerial)

here buttercups shall
robin out the thread
that led beyond the
furcoat pleasures of a night
here gopher lights
shall fall and crawl
from one small suitcab
built for two

and now the shell holes
dwindle into fences
white as cherry lit with
snow
or carcassonned in
strength unyoked to
ivory plants that
turquoise airily to sea
(the waves are paper

bags to burst)
up that great Step to Sun
  (zythum to aardvark
      and back again)
here xebecs tell of toadstools
tabled out in pride
here xebecs tell of one lost bride
whose solaced eyes once
wept
to see the bursting parasols
migrate
between the two necessities of life

  (and if her tossing hair
should catch
upon an edge of cloud)

and hearts in fear inurned
murmur here name
and dream sharp arrows
squeezed to stick upon
the Target of Sun

or play at proposition
with the maid who gilly-gillies to the
S of mountain
railroad tracks
or rides astride their backs
voluptual as books in June

and in my bed
the Mad Queen lies
the Mad Queen of the bedroom eyes
the Idol I idolatrize

   Color explodes
where once the feet of
Tripod Time danced wantonly
   to bugle notes
(of unremembered telephones)

queer Goya tailcoats
   sneezing into soot
queer rabbits falling
   from the Flagpole of the year

and breasts spurt flowers
   cramoisy and dark
and nestling turtledoves
   are seen through fog

beyond the crow-black roads

   Color Explodes

and if a proper noun
invigorates our teeth

  can we not say
     Black Black
         I wake to Sun !

[*An Anthology of the Younger Poets,* 1932]

Poems from Chariot of the Sun
(1928)

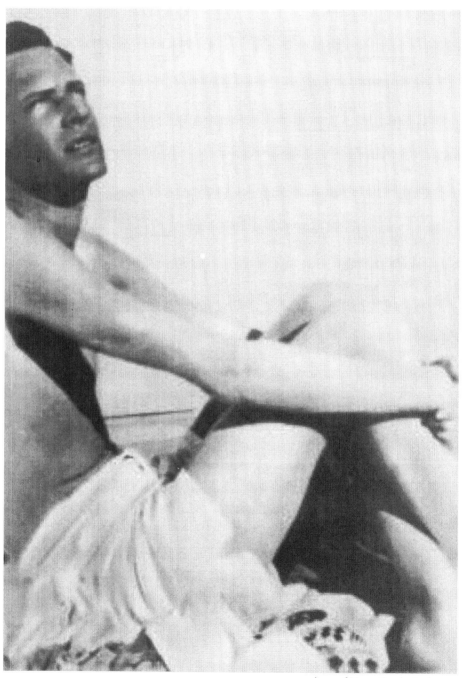

photo of Harry Crosby in the sun

STUDY FOR A SOUL

the colors have begun to form
silvergray with cramoisy and gold
into an arrow carved by storm
beyond the fear or new and old

and where the arrow fits the bow
the untroubled darkness of her eyes
watches the red-gold target grow—
strong is the Sun that purifies

but I have sought in vain to find
the riddle of the bow and archer
there were not shadows left behind
after the heart's departure.

SUN RHAPSODY

The Sun ! The Sun !

a fish in the aquarium of sky
or golden net to snare the butterfly
of soul
        or else the hole
through which the stars have disappeared

it is a forest without trees
it is a lion in a cage of breeze
it is the roundness of her knees
great Hercules
and all the seas
and our soliloquies

winter-cold anchorite
summer-hot sybarite
to-day a lady wrapped in clouds
to-morrow hunted by the hungry clouds

it is a monster that our thoughts have speared
the Queen we chanticleered

a mother's womb
a child's balloon
red burning tomb

TOUGGOURT

An Arab beating monotonously upon a drum, the tuneless and persistent wailing of the flutes and the dancing Ouled-Nails, their limbs bronzed by the sun and their nipples like silver fruit.

Handmaidens of the Sun.

And the waving palm trees and the camels in the Sahara bringing in brushwood, swaying like Dunsany Wood —

And the caravan and the caravanserai and the burning suns of the desert —

Splendor Solis, Sol the Roman God of the Sun, the Giant Pyramid of the Sun, The Virgins of the Sun in Peru, Sun-Worship.

PHOTOHELIOGRAPH

(for Lady A.)

black black black black black
black black black black black
black black black black black
black black black black black
black black SUN black black
black black black black black
black black black black black
black black black black black
black black black black black
black black black black black

TREE OF GOLD

Xairo (I rejoice)
naked in the sun
under the sun-clouds formed like skulls

and a bateau-mouche
thrusting under the arch of a bridge
is a silver thread
        drawn by invisible fingers
through a gold needle
(or a silver soul
        threading a gold body

and the train of barges
(gold leviathans)
under the bridge of jade
under the bridge of rose -colored marble
and beyond—down down beyond
under the bridge of sunstone
and beyond—

were it not for the Abyss
there would be no need for bridges
no need
for the sun-triumphant arches of the soul
no need
for sunsets seen at dawn

the Sun's reflection in the water
is a tree of gold
and the arches of the bridges
are windows to the sea

and at sunset
windows to the sun.
a last faint touch of gold
the no-more tree of gold
the blackness of the river
swallows gold

among the river of the soul
in mirrored ecstasy the Sun
the new-born tree of gold
erects its dome of rainbow-colored leaves
and like the throbbing of a violin
heard in the heart long after it has ceased
or lover from strange darknesses released
untroubled, dreams the body it deceives.

PSYCHOPATHIA SEXUALIS

(Case 19)

X., peasant, aged thirty-four and a half; Sun-Worshipper. Father and Mother were hard drinkers. Since his fifth year patient has had epileptic convulsions — i.e. he falls down unconscious, lies still two or three minutes, and then gets up and runs directly with staring eyes towards the Sun. Sexuality was first manifested at seventeen. The patient had inclinations neither for women nor for men, but for constellations (stars, moons, suns etcetera) He had intercourse with stars and moons and later with comets and suns. Never any onanism.

The patient paints pictures of suns; is of a very limited intelligence : For years, religious paranoia, with states of ecstasy. He has an " inexplicable " love for the Sun, for whom he would sacrifice his life. Taken to hospital, he proves to be free from infirmity and signs of anatomical degeneration.

FRAGMENT OF AN ETUDE FOR A SUN-DIAL

                let the Sun shine
                (and the Sun shone)
on a wooden dial
in the garden of an old castle
(dumb when the Sun is dark)

on a pillar dial
in the cimetiere de l'Abbaye de Longchamp
(blessed be the name of the Sun for all ages)

on the wall of an imaginary house
Rue du Soleil Paris
(the initials of the makers H.C. and C.C. and date
October Seventh 1927 are on the face)
(true as the dial to the Sun)

on a small stone dial
over the door of a farm
(sole oriente orior
sole ponente cubo)

on the exterior of a ring dial
worn on the finger of the Princess Jacqueline
(" Es-tu donc le Soleil pour vouloir que je me tourne
vers Toi ")

on the dial of the south wall
        of a tower
(the Sun is the end of the journey)

and there is a second dial
    on the north wall
(I tarry not for the slow)

on a dial
over an archway in a stableyard
(norma del tempo infallible io sono)
(I am the infallible measure of the time)

on a dial
in a garden in Malta

on a dial at Versailles

on an old Spanish dial
(the dial has now, 1928, disappeared a railroad line
having been taken through the garden where it stood)

on the wall of the
Bar de la Tempete at
Brest facing the sea
(c'est l'heure de boire)

on a small brass dial in
   the British Museum
on a silver dial in the
   Museum at Copenhagen
on a gold dial in the
   soul of a Girl
(" mais à mon âme la nécessité de ton âme ")

       let the Sun shine
       (and the Sun shone)

on a dial placed upon the
deck of the Aeolus
in the harbor of New London.
on a dial placed upon the
deck of the Aphrodisiac
in the harbor of Brest
on a dial placed upon
the deck of the Aurora
in the harbor of my Heart
(" et quelques-uns en eurent connaissance ")

       let the Sun shine
       (and the Sun shone)

on pyramids of stones
on upright stones in
ancient graveyards
on upright solitary stones
on bones white-scattered on the plain
the white bones of lions in the sun
the white lion is the phallus of the Sun
" I am the Lions I am the Sun "

on the dial of Ahaz who
reigned over Judah

on a rude horologe in Egypt
(" as a servant earnestly

desireth the shadow")

on the eight dials of
the Tower of the Winds at Athens

on old Roman coins
unburied from the ground

on the twin sundials on
the ramparts of Carcassonne

on the pier at Sunderland
(and where is the sound
      of the pendulum)

on the sun-dials on the mosques
    of Saint Sophia
    of Muhammed
and of Sulimania

on the immense circular
block of carved porphyry
in the Great Square of
the City of Mexico

on Aztec dials

on Inca dials
(Femme offre ton soleil en adoration aux Incas)

on Teutonic dials built

into the walls of
old churches

on the dial of the Durer Melancholia
(above the hour-glass and near the bell)

on the white marble slab
which projects from the
facade of Santa Maria Della Salute
on the Grand Canal Venice

on the dial of the Cathedral at Chartres
(" the strong wind and the snows ")

on a bedstead made of bronze
(and Heliogabalus had one of solid silver)

on a marriage bed
(lectus genialis)
on a death bed
(lectus funebrius)

on a bed
style à la marquis
(" ayant peur de mourir lorsque je couche seul ")

on a bed
lit d'ange

on a flower bed
on a bed of mother-of-pearl

on a bordel bed
on a bed of iniquity
on a virgin bed
on a bed of rock

(To God the Sun Unconquerable)
to the peerless sun, we only

       let the Sun shine
       (and the Sun shone)

       Soli Soli Soli

Poems from Transit of Venus (1929)

wedding photo of Harry and Caresse Crosby

FIRST MEETING

*(" lorsque Vénus est tout
entière entrée dans le disque ")*

When you are the flower
I am the shadow cast by the flower
When I am the fire
You are the mirror reflecting the fire
And when Venus has entered the disk of the Sun
Then you are that Venus and I am the Sun.

ALTAZIMUTH

We know not what we may
(Graves of princesses
Green in our souls)
By rockets and flashing of signals
By trigonometrical surveys
By the aid of chronometers
By ultra-violet rays
We know not what we may erect
By transit observations of the moon,
By culminating stars, soon,
By the aid of an altazimuth
We shall erect
Perpendiculars enough.

YOU CAME TO ME

You came to me
On all the winds of an ostrich,
On winds of the desert,
On evening wind
Of night, falls from the
Of silence, float upon the
Of morning,
On the wind, fly upon the
Of winds came flying on,
On wide-waving,
Sailing on echo
Of winds.

POEM

The moon, as yon dead,
The rolling,
The whole kin
The whole wide
There is not in the wide
This great roundabout
This gross, hard-seeming,
This my,
This little
This pendent
This unintelligible,
Thou art the whole wide,
Three corners of the
Tired of wandering orbit.

YOUTH

Fair, all that is, by nature good,
Crystal river
Ever young and strong,
Man that has his quiver full
Ever young and strong,
And good as she,
And never wrong,
He softly goes
With unpolluted flesh
To gather petals from the rose.

YOUR KISS

I am —
It was your kiss that made me
Gather bright arrows
For the day of death
A death more beautiful than death
A fire upon fire
Behold your beauty carrying fire —
Apparition seen and gone
Cannot make the prospect less
Summer with Autumn shall undress.

BE NOT IT IS I

Be not, it is I
Whistling to keep from being
On our dull side
Fleeing to ocean
Come never back
Cut and come
Flow gently sweet
Looking before and
Of her best days
Sunshine asleep,
Come never back
Cut and come —
Us the deluge
Which has come.

WERE IT NOT BETTER

Were it not better, not too soon,
On even keel, though it be dark,
On life's dark ocean, for us to sail
On O ship of state (unmockingly)
(We know not where we go)
On I gold bark of the moon
(O Bay of Biscay,
O to be a wolf and bay the moon)
On O Union strong and great
Set every threadbare swan
Upon the sea
Mate with the many mermaids, go
Loved by you and loved by me
      To and fro
To love and not to
      Sink below.

PRAYER

Day, from darkness to
Day, lead me O Sun till
Days, unto the
Day, then if ever come
Days which weigh upon the heart,
Lead me quietly away
Lead me quietly apart.

THAT HARD WORD

That hard word
That sore saying spoken
The end —
The poor creature, I do,
The power of beauty, I,
The way we parted
Forget that I,
I cannot, but that such things were,
I remember (broken-hearted)
Only Her.

LOST THINGS

Lost things
Were warm with beauty
Bird of the
Birds of the have nests
Her charming gestures and her breasts
Hurtle in the darkened room,
So soft, so hushed,
So soft the birds in nests,
So soft her breasts.

BEAUTY IN BED

All her sorrow, all her
All in vain,
And ashes
And laughter
And smiles, kisses
Are shed
Beauty smiling in her bed.

LITTLE POEMS

I

Two dark little doors
    (Her eyes).

II

    Her ears
Two little slippers
For the feet of my voice.

KISS

This blessed fruit, this,
This goodly red,
This fire, this O, this.
This is the last of
This kiss.

FIRE-EATERS

At every one in his castle
(moonlight sleeps upon the
bed of violets, breathes upon a
shoal of time,
better for being a little
over-sublime)
At every one at his feasting
At Kings and Queens at their feast
We laugh on our bed of laughter
Because we are least
(the ruin lay, lovely in death
the ruin lies, and
lovers admire
her naked eyes)
Viler than vile esteemed
Because we devour the fire
Others have dreamed.

FORECAST

I care not
If Fortune is blind, fickle
Is like glass,
Has divers ways,
Is unstable,
Is on our side, when,
Is false as brass,
Leads on to,
Leaves some door open,
Favors bridegroom or bride,
Sees love-words broken.

I only care
Lest Fortune mar
(then I shall be particular)
Your bare, bright beauty
Slings and arrows
To make you common as the sparrows.

AND MEMORY

And memory
At which the soul grew pale —
I thus leave thee
Not what we would
But what we live without —
O nightingale
We will not ask her
Of her face,
By man,
By strangers,
By the midnight place
Where beauty rustles in the dark,
Revered and honored,
Loved and lost,
Far-hidden in the heart
Of gallant men,
Of soldiers slain,
Of shipwrecked poets
In the rain.

YES

One little
One golden
Of bliss winged
With flying feet
One vision golden
Of the sun and sea
One precise moment
Of clarity.

Poems from Torchbearer (1931)

photo of Kay Boyle and Harry Crosby

ACADEMY OF STIMULANTS

Do you know what an explosion is or a madness? Do you know the three great elements in an attack? Do you know the voltage required to create a current between the artery of the heart and the Sun?

TATTOO

I am the criminal whose chest is tattooed with a poinard above which are graven the words " mort aux bourgeois ". Let us each tattoo this on our hearts.

I am the soldier with a red mark on my nakedness — when in a frenzy of love the mark expands to spell Mad Queen. Let us each tattoo our Mad Queen on our heart.

I am the prophet from the land of the Sun whose back is tattooed in the design of a rising run. Let us each tattoo a rising sun on our heart.

I DRINK TO THE SUN

Mad day flags crackling in the dawn the sharp intensity of drink dentelleries thrown over the mill fire sun and candlelight and at midnight I squeeze the juice of the silver fruit of the moon into the red glass of my heart. I drink to the Sun who lies concealed in his bed under the sheets of night. In the morning he will rise like a Red Indian to run his marathon across the sky.

ASSASSIN

" Voici le temps des assassins…"
Rimbaud

    I exchange eyes with the Mad Queen.
    The mirror crashes against my face and bursts into a thousand suns. All over the city flags crackle and bang. Foghorns scream in the harbor. The wind hurricanes through the window. Tornadoes are unmuzzled as I begin to dance the dance of the Kurd Shepherds.
    I stamp upon the floor. I whirl like dervishes. Colors revolve dressing and undressing. I lash them with fury stark white with iron black harsh red with blue marble green with bright orange and only gold remains naked. I roar with joy.
    Black-footed ferrets disappear into holes.
    The sun tattooed on my back begins to spin faster and faster whirring whirring throwing out a glory of sparks. Sparks shoot off into space sparks into shooting stars. Shooting stars collide with comets. Explosions. Naked colors explode into Red Disaster.
    I crash out through a window naked widespread upon a Heliosaurus. I up root an obelisk and plunge it into the ink-pot of the Black Sea. I write the word SUN across the dreary palimpsest of the world. I pour the contents of the Red Sea down my throat. I erect catapults and lay siege to the cities of the world. I scatter violent disorder throughout the kingdoms of the world. I stone the people of the world. I stride over mountains. I pick up oceans like thin cards and spin them into oblivion. I kick down walled cities. I hurl giant firebrands against governments. I thrust torches through the eyes of the law.
    I annihilate museums. I demolish libraries. I oblivionize skyscrapers.

I become hard as adamant strong as battle indurated with solid fire rigid with hatred.

I bring back the wizards and the sorcerers the necromancers the magicians. O practice witchcraft. I set up idols. With a sharp-edged sword I cut through the crowded streets. Comets follow in my wake. Stars make obeisance to me. The moon uncovers her nakedness to me.

I am the harbinger of a New Sun World. I bring the seed of a New Copulation. I proclaim the Mad Queen.

I stamp out vast empires. I crush palaces in my rigid hands. I harden my heart against churches.

I blot out cemeteries. I feed the people with stinging nettles. I resurrect madness. I thrust my naked sword between the ribs of the world. I murder the world !

FOR YOU

I am the paralune for you to hide behind. I do not wish you frozen by the moon.

I am the chariot of fire for you to ride upon to Sun.

INFURIATE

" unleash the sword and fire "
Shelley

I annihilate. I assassinate. I infuriate myself against the herd. I prognosticate the Bird of the Sun. I take cardiac and aphrodisiac. I become maniac and demoniac. I run towards the Maddest Queen. I precipitate myself through Stars to find my Dream.

UNLEASH THE HOUNDS

They play at their game of croquet but there is no queen to shout " get to your places " no hedgehogs for balls no live flamingos for mallets no soldiers to stand upon their hands and feet to make the arches — so is the game of life a very ordinary game unless we unleash the hounds of imagination.

STRONG FOR BATTLE

Five requisites necessary : madness, the strength to attack (I summon you O warriors of my Foreign Legion), a prearranged system of explosions, a vast supply of gold (to extract each day an ingot of gold from the quarry of sun), a hard training for the last chariot-race and my horses shall be Comet and Meteor.

GLADNESS

Glad the landmarks have been swallowed in the ocean, glad the worm shall feed upon Philistines, glad the Sun has thrust his phallic fire into the womb of my soul.

ALLEGORY

I stand on the prow of a viking ship far out on the Sea of Beyond under a sky of emerald dreams — a leviathan with explosions for eyes and nostrils snorting destruction furrows past with the strength of turbines — as he tornados over the horizon the sea turns into a black mirror. I see a rainbow-nymph widespread upon a dolphin surge past in the opposite direction to the leviathan. Battleships emerge painted silver and gold. They are shaped like arrows. Pirate junks in the shape of stars fly the skull and crossbones. Soot-colored fishing-smacks are the shape of shields. Red icebergs drift like tombs across the Sun. With a gold sword I trace upon a block of silver the red words of War. I enclose this poem in an iron casket blacker than the mirror and with black chains I lower it into the mirror until it is engulfed in the mirror — then suddenly the Dawn the mirror fades into a flutter of foam and I am precipitated by a diamond wind in pursuit of the Nymph.

A knock on the door — il est sept heures, Monsieur.

TIDAL WAVE

There is a sun that plunges this evening a red phallus into the womb of the sea and there are seagulls upon the rim of a floating buoy like thought-pearls upon the black coronet of the brain and there is the tide in one continuous incoming wave sweeping in over the sands faster than my legs can run. O tide-producing force tending to deform the body. O tides of the sea ! O tides of the Sun !

illustration by Alastair
from *Red Skeletons*

Textual Notes

Poems from *transition*

HAIL : DEATH !
As "Sun-Death" in MAD QUEEN.

SUITE
AERONAUTICS
MAD QUEEN.

THE SUN
As "Madman" in MAD QUEEN.

THE NEW WORD
Not collected.

OBSERVATION-POST
Not collected.

DREAMS 1928–1929
1
As "Glass Princess" in SLEEPING TOGETHER.

2
See p. 106. As "Cue of Wind" in SLEEPING TOGETHER.

3
See p. 70. As "We Have Forgotten Our Calling-Cards" in SLEEPING TOGETHER.

4
See p. 87. As "Dice in a Yellow Skull" in SLEEPING TOGETHER.

5
See p. 78. As "Naked Lady in a Yellow Hat" in SLEEPING TOGETHER.

6
See p. 73. As "Cat" in *SLEEPING TOGETHER*.

7
See p. 85. As "Aeronautics" in *SLEEPING TOGETHER*.

8
See p. 74. As "They the Twelve Lions" in *SLEEPING TOGETHER*.

9
See p. 69. As "Girls Under Ten" in *SLEEPING TOGETHER*.

10
See p. 75. As "One Hundred Ways of Kissing Girls" in *SLEEPING TOGETHER*.

11
See p. 78. As "C C" in *SLEEPING TOGETHER*.

12
See p. 81. As "Queen of Hearts" in *SLEEPING TOGETHER*.

13
See p. 72. As "I am in Your Soul" in *SLEEPING TOGETHER*.

14
See p. 155. As "Allegory" in *TORCHBEARER*.

15
Not collected.

16
See p. 83. As "The Red Umbrella" in *SLEEPING TOGETHER*.

17
See p. 70. As "On the Grounds of Indecency" in *SLEEPING TOGETHER*.

18
See p. 92. As "Ritz Tower" in SLEEPING TOGETHER.

19
See p. 75. As "Sunrise Express" in SLEEPING TOGETHER.

20
Not collected.

21
See p. 93. As "In Pursuit of Your Eyes" in SLEEPING TOGETHER.

22
See p. 72. As "Unremoved by Rubbing" in SLEEPING TOGETHER.

23
Not collected.

FOR A PROTECTION
See pp. 37, 90. SLEEPING TOGETHER.

ILLUSTRATIONS OF MADNESS

1
Not collected.

2
Not collected.

3
Not collected.

4
Not collected.

5
Not collected.

6
Not collected.

7
Not collected.

8
Not collected.

9
Not collected.

10
Not collected.

SHORT INTRODUCTION TO THE WORD

1
Not collected.

2
Not collected.

3
Not collected.

4
Not collected.

5
Not collected.

6
Not collected.

7
Not collected.

8
Not collected.

SLEEPING TOGETHER

FOR A PROTECTION
See pp. 31, 90. *SLEEPING TOGETHER.*

WHITE SLIPPER
See p. 92. *SLEEPING TOGETHER.*

WHITE CLOVER
See p. 87. *SLEEPING TOGETHER.*

SAFETY-PIN
See p. 83. *SLEEPING TOGETHER.*

HUMAN FLESH AND GOLDEN APPLES
See p. 85. *SLEEPING TOGETHER.*

I BREAK WITH THE PAST
See p. 89. *SLEEPING TOGETHER.*

GOLDEN SPOON
See p. 90. *SLEEPING TOGETHER.*

AUNT AGATHA
See p. 91. *SLEEPING TOGETHER.*

IT IS SNOWING
See p. 79. *SLEEPING TOGETHER.*

WHITE AEROPLANES IN FLIGHT
See p. 77. *SLEEPING TOGETHER.*

MIRACULOUS MESSAGE
See p. 76. *SLEEPING TOGETHER.*

EMBRACE ME YOU SAID
SLEEPING TOGETHER.

A PROGRESS UPWARD
See p. 82. *SLEEPING TOGETHER.*

WHITE FIRE
See p. 91. *SLEEPING TOGETHER.*

REVIRGINATE
See p. 84. *SLEEPING TOGETHER.*

ANIMAL MAGNETISM
See p. 77. SLEEPING TOGETHER.

Poems from The Decachord, Blues, The Morada, Pagany, and Four Anthologies

OUR LADY OF TEARS

BILITIS

TRUMPET OF DEPARTURE
TORCHBEARER.

SCORN
See p. 68. *TORCHBEARER.*

DESOLATE
Not collected.

103°
TORCHBEARER.

ASSASSIN
See p. 148. *MAD QUEEN; TORCHBEARER.*

THE ROSE
TRANSIT OF VENUS.

OUR FEET
As "Feet of the Sun" in *TRANSIT OF VENUS.*

SLEEPING TOGETHER
As "Last Contact" in *TRANSIT OF VENUS.*

SHARING FIRE
TRANSIT OF VENUS.

ROOTS
TRANSIT OF VENUS.

CŒUR DE JEUNE FEMME
TRANSIT OF VENUS.

VENUS
TRANSIT OF VENUS.

MIRACLE
TRANSIT OF VENUS.

RECKON THE DAYS
TRANSIT OF VENUS.

INVOCATION TO THE SUN-GODDESS
See p. 96. As "Invocation to the Mad Queen" in *MAD QUEEN.*

SCORN
See p. 51. *TORCHBEARER.*

SLEEPING TOGETHER
A BOOK OF DREAMS

INSPECTION
SLEEPING TOGETHER.

GIRLS UNDER TEN
See p. 26. *SLEEPING TOGETHER.*

ON THE GROUNDS OF INDECENCY
See p. 28. *SLEEPING TOGETHER.*

WE HAVE FORGOTTEN OUR CALLING-CARDS
See p. 24. *SLEEPING TOGETHER.*

NO INDICATION OF WHERE I MIGHT FIND YOU
SLEEPING TOGETHER.

GAME OF TAG
SLEEPING TOGETHER.

PERFORMANCE BY TWO
SLEEPING TOGETHER.

I AM IN YOUR SOUL
See p. 27. *SLEEPING TOGETHER.*

UNREMOVED BY RUBBING
See p. 29. *SLEEPING TOGETHER.*

MOSQUITO
SLEEPING TOGETHER.

OVID'S FLEA
SLEEPING TOGETHER.

CAT
See p. 25. *SLEEPING TOGETHER.*

GAZELLE AT LUNCHEON
SLEEPING TOGETHER.

THEY THE TWELVE LIONS
See p. 26. *SLEEPING TOGETHER.*

ONE HUNDRED WAYS OF KISSING GIRLS
See p. 26. *SLEEPING TOGETHER.*

SUNRISE EXPRESS
See p. 29. *SLEEPING TOGETHER.*

I HAD NO IDEA WHAT THEY WOULD DO NEXT
SLEEPING TOGETHER.

HE CALLED US A GIRL
SLEEPING TOGETHER.

MIRACULOUS MESSAGE
See p. 41. *SLEEPING TOGETHER.*

WHITE AEROPLANES IN FLIGHT
See p. 41. *SLEEPING TOGETHER.*

ANIMAL MAGNETISM
See p. 43. *SLEEPING TOGETHER.*

SAINT VALENTINE'S NIGHT
SLEEPING TOGETHER.

YOUR EYES ARE THE REAL EYES
SLEEPING TOGETHER.

NAKED LADY IN A YELLOW HAT
See p. 25. *SLEEPING TOGETHER.*

CUE OF WIND
See p. 24. *SLEEPING TOGETHER.*

C C
See p. 26. *SLEEPING TOGETHER.*

IT IS SNOWING
See p. 40. *SLEEPING TOGETHER.*

VERY NICE TO LOOK AT AND SWEET TO TOUCH
SLEEPING TOGETHER.

YOU ARE STANDING ON YOUR HEAD
SLEEPING TOGETHER.

STREET OF THE FOUR WINDS
SLEEPING TOGETHER.

QUEEN OF HEARTS
See p. 27. *SLEEPING TOGETHER.*

WHITE ERMINE
SLEEPING TOGETHER.

MIRACLE OF THE TOOTH
SLEEPING TOGETHER.

C PREFERRED
SLEEPING TOGETHER.

A PROGRESS UPWARD
See p. 42. *SLEEPING TOGETHER.*

THE RED UMBRELLA
See p. 28. *SLEEPING TOGETHER.*

I WAS NEVER HAPPIER
SLEEPING TOGETHER.

SAFETY-PIN
See p. 38. *SLEEPING TOGETHER.*

SOLUTION OF A MYSTERY
SLEEPING TOGETHER.

REVIRGINATE
SLEEPING TOGETHER.

HUMAN FLESH AND GOLDEN APPLES
See p. 38. *SLEEPING TOGETHER.*

AERONAUTICS
SLEEPING TOGETHER.

GIRLS ARE CLIMBING
SLEEPING TOGETHER.

YOU WERE TRYING TO TELL ME SOMETHING
SLEEPING TOGETHER.

THE CRAMOISY QUEEN
SLEEPING TOGETHER.

DICE IN A YELLOW SKULL
See p. 25. *SLEEPING TOGETHER.*

WHITE CLOVER
SLEEPING TOGETHER.

CRUEL MOUTH AND LITTLE EAR
SLEEPING TOGETHER.

I FOLLOW YOU TO BED
SLEEPING TOGETHER.

FOR THE PREVENTION OF CRUELTY TO BRIDES
SLEEPING TOGETHER.

I BREAK WITH THE PAST
See p. 39. *SLEEPING TOGETHER.*

GOLDEN SPOON
See p. 39. *SLEEPING TOGETHER.*

SEESAW
SLEEPING TOGETHER.

FOR A PROTECTION
See pp. 31, 37. *SLEEPING TOGETHER.*

WHITE FIRE
See p. 43. *SLEEPING TOGETHER.*

AUNT AGATHA
See p. 40. *SLEEPING TOGETHER.*

RITZ TOWER
See p. 28. *SLEEPING TOGETHER.*

WHITE STOCKINGS
SLEEPING TOGETHER.

WHITE SLIPPER
See p. 37. *SLEEPING TOGETHER.*

ONE LETTER OF THE ALPHABET
SLEEPING TOGETHER.

IN PURSUIT OF YOUR EYES
SLEEPING TOGETHER.

HORSE RACE
MAD QUEEN.

INVOCATION TO THE MAD QUEEN
See p. 67. *MAD QUEEN.*

IN MADNESS
MAD QUEEN.

EMPTY BED BLUES
MAD QUEEN.

WATER-LILIES
CHARIOT OF THE SUN.

QUATRAINS TO THE SUN
CHARIOT OF THE SUN.

SUNSTROKE
MAD QUEEN.

illustration by Alastair
from *Red Skeletons*

Bibliography

Books by Harry Crosby

Anthology. As by Henry Grew Crosby. [Paris]: Privately printed, probably early in 1924.

Sonnets for Caresse. First edition. Paris: n.p., 1925. 17 copies.

Sonnets for Caresse. Second edition. Paris: n.p., 1926. 27 copies.

Sonnets for Caresse. Third edition. Paris: Albert Messein, 1926. 107 copies.

Sonnets for Caresse. Fourth edition. Paris: Editions Narcisse, 1927. 44 copies.

Red Skeletons. Paris: Editions Narcisse, 1927. First book to be printed by Lescaret under the direction of the Crosbys. 370 copies.

Chariot of the Sun. Paris: At The Sign of the Sundial, Cour Du Soleil D'Or, 1928. 48 copies issued.

Shadows of the Sun. First edition. Paris: The Black Sun Press, 1928. First book to bear the Black Sun imprint. Edition limited to 44 copies.

Transit of Venus. First edition. Paris: The Black Sun Press, Editions Narcisse, 1928. Edition limited to 44 copies.

Transit of Venus. Second edition. Paris: The Black Sun Press, 1929. Edition limited to 200 copies.

Mad Queen : Tirades. First edition. Paris: The Black Sun Press, Editions Narcisse, 1929. 141 copies printed for commerce.

Shadows of the Sun (Second Series). First edition. Paris: The Black Sun Press, 1929. Edition limited to 44 copies.

The Sun. Paris: The Black Sun Press, 1929. Edition limited to 100 copies.

Sleeping Together: A Book of Dreams. First edition. Paris: The Black Sun Press, 1929. Edition limited to 77 copies.

Shadows of the Sun (Third Series). Paris: The Black Sun Press, 1930.

Aphrodite in Flight: Being Some Observations On The Aerodynamics of Love. Paris: The Black Sun Press, 1930. Edition limited to 27 copies.

Chariot of the Sun (Collected Poems of Harry Crosby). Introduction by D.H. Lawrence. Paris: The Black Sun Press, 1931. Edition limited to 570 copies.

Transit of Venus (Collected Poems of Harry Crosby). Preface by T.S. Eliot. Paris: The Black Sun Press, 1931. Edition limited to 570 copies.

Sleeping Together (Collected Poems of Harry Crosby). With a Memory of the Poet by Stuart Gilbert. Paris: The Black Sun Press, 1931. Edition limited to 570 copies.

Torchbearer (Collected Poems of Harry Crosby). With Notes by Ezra Pound. Paris: The Black Sun Press, 1931. Edition limited to 570 copies.

War Letters. First edition. As by Henry Grew Crosby. Paris: The Black Sun Press, 1932. Privately printed edition limited to 125 copies.

Shadows of the Sun: The Diaries of Harry Crosby. Ed. by Edward Germain. Santa Barbara: Black Sparrow Press, 1977.

Periodicals Containing Contributions by Harry Crosby

transition 14, Fall 1928.

transition 15, February 1929.

transition 16-17, June 1929.

transition 18, November 1929.

transition 19–20, June 1930. Harry Crosby Feature.

The Decachord, Vol. IV, No. 15, March–April 1928.

The Decachord, Vol. V, No. 20, November–December 1929.

Blues, Vol. I, No. 5, 1929.

Blues, Vol. I, No. 6, 1929.

The Morada 1, Fall 1929.

The Morada 2, Winter 1930. Harry Crosby number.

Pagany, Vol. I, No. I, Winter 1930.

The Hound and Horn, Vol. III, No. 2, Winter 1930. Three Crosby photographs.

Portfolio I, The Black Sun Press, Summer 1945. 1,300 copies issued. One Crosby photograph.

Portfolio V, The Black Sun Press, Spring 1947. Deluxe copies limited to 200. Eight poems from *Transit of Venus*.

Anthologies Containing Contributions by Harry Crosby

Unrest: The Rebel Poets' Anthology for 1929. Ed. by Ralph Cheney and Jack Conroy. London: Arthur H. Stockwell, Ltd., 1929.

Unrest: The Rebel Poets' Anthology for 1930. Ed. by Ralph Cheney and Jack Conroy. London : 'Studies' Publications, 1930.

American Caravan IV. Ed. by Alfred Kreymborg, Lewis Mumford, and Paul Rosenfeld. New York: The Macauley Company, 1931.

An Anthology of the Younger Poets. Ed. by Oliver Wells. Philadelphia: The Centaur Press, 1932.

Americans Abroad: An Anthology. Ed. by Peter Neagoe. The Hague: The Servire Press, 1932. Selections from Shadows of the Sun.

Transition Workshop. Ed. by Eugene Jolas. New York: Vanguard Press, 1949.

Further Reading

Cowley, Malcolm. *Exile's Return: A Narrative of Ideas*. New York: W.W. Norton & Company, Inc., 1934.

The Letters of Hart Crane: 1916–1932. Ed. by Brom Weber. New York: Hermitage House, 1952.

Crosby, Caresse. *The Passionate Years*. New York: The Dial Press, 1953.

Horton, Philip. *Hart Crane: The Life of An American Poet*. New York: W.W. Norton & Company, Inc., 1937.

Minkoff, George Robert. *A Bibliography of The Black Sun Press*. Introduction by Caresse Crosby. Great Neck, NY: G.R. Minkoff, 1970.

Rothenberg, Jerome, Ed. *Revolution of the Word: A New Gathering of American Avant-Garde Poetry*, 1914–1945. Boston: Exact Change, 2004.

Unterecker, John. *Voyager: A Life of Hart Crane*. New York: Farrar, Straus, and Giroux, 1969,

Wolff, Geoffrey. *Black Sun: The Brief Transit and Violent Eclipse of Harry Crosby*. New York: Ransom House, 1976.

Acknowledgments

I wish to thank the following individuals and institutions for assistance in the preparation of this volume: The Houghton Library, Harvard University, The Boston Athenaeum, Strand Book Store, Sylvia Petras, Leaf and Stone Books, Ed Smith, Ed Smith Books, Terry Halliday, William Reese Company, Pamela Sue Hackbart-Dean, Director, Morris Library Special Collections, Southern Illinois University at Carbondale, Mary Warnement, Natalie Zimmerman, Shannon Supple, Nichole Calero, Smith College Special Collections, Lesley Brooks, Woburn Books, Madison Glassmyer, Mullen Books, Daniel Adams, Waverley Books, Elizabeth Doran, Grolier Poetry Book Shop, James Dunn, Suzanne Mercury, Stephen Sturgeon, Philip Nikolayev, Marc Vincenz, Rob Chalfen, Susan Dickey, John Howard, Harvey Mazer, Peter Behrman de Sinéty, Petya Ivanova, Sawsan El-Ayoubi, Robert Archambeau, Ruth Lepson, Mario Murgia, John Mulrooney, Eliot Cardinaux, and Paul S. Rowe. Above all I wish to thank Morris Library Special Collections, Southern Illinois University at Carbondale, for permission to publish Harry Crosby's poems.

An abridged version of the Introduction to this book was published in *Lit Hub*. Thanks to Aaron Robertson.

About the Editor

BEN MAZER was born in New York City in 1964. He was educated at Harvard University, where he studied with Seamus Heaney and William Alfred, and at the Editorial Institute, Boston University, where his advisors were Christopher Ricks and Archie Burnett. He is the author of several collections of poems, including *White Cities* (Barbara Matteau Editions, 1995), *Poems* (Pen & Anvil Press, 2010), *January 2008* (Dark Sky Books, 2010), *New Poems* (Pen & Anvil Press, 2013), *The Glass Piano* (MadHat Press, 2015), *December Poems* (Pen & Anvil Press, 2016), *February Poems* (Ilora Press, 2017), and *Selected Poems* (MadHat Press, 2017). He is the editor of *The Collected Poems of John Crowe Ransom* (Un-Gyve Press, 2015), *Selected Poems of Frederick Goddard Tuckerman* (Harvard University Press, 2010), *The Uncollected Delmore Schwartz* (Arrowsmith Press, 2019), and Landis Everson's *Everything Preserved: Poems 1955–2005* (Graywolf Press, 2006), which won the first Emily Dickinson Award from the Poetry Foundation. Formerly the editor of *The Battersea Review*, he lives in Cambridge, Massachusetts, and is co-editor, with Raquel Balboni, of *Art and Letters*. He is currently editing *The Collected Poems of Delmore Schwartz* for Farrar Straus & Giroux.

Made in the USA
Middletown, DE
31 May 2023